GW01003395

NUDES
BREAKFAST:

STEYNING GRAMMAR SCHOOL
DURING THE SECOND WORLD WAR.

GEORGE BARKER

GEORGE BARKER
8 Chapel Street,
Warmington PE8 6TR

NUDES AT BREAKFAST

ISBN 978-0-9540342-1-4

First published in October 2009 by:

GEORGE BARKER
8 Chapel Street,
Warmington PE8 6TR

Designed and printed in Great Britain by Inkwell Printing Ltd
www.inkwellprinting.co.uk

Dedication

To all the staff of the haematology and oncology Clinics at Peterborough District Hospital who, during sessions of chemotherapy cheered me on with wit and humour when I brought in swathes of documents with me to research this volume.

Also to the late Jean Scragg who, above all others encouraged me in recording what took place at Steyning Grammar School until its integration with the present Comprehensive School in 1968.

Acknowledgements

Over the past nine years I have been privileged to meet as individuals, or in small groups, Steyning Grammar School Old Boys who have vivid recollections of the immediate pre-war, post-war and war years. They are among those remaining who do indeed grow old and whom age does begin to weary and the years condemn. Their stories are worth telling and worth saving. In the classification system adopted by authors, most fall into that convenient sub-group of 'Those Too Numerous to Mention'. In this account I draw freely on their conversations, letters and memoirs, supplemented with information from the Steyning Museum archives and published material ranging from local leaflets to standard texts, all of which are listed under references for those with enquiring minds.

The illustrations come from the archive of photos and documents contributed by Old Boys and from the archives of Steyning Museum. I am grateful to the Museum for letting me cherry-pick photos from the collection and to all the Old Boys whose contributions have been used here.

Of the many people who have been involved in gathering material and stimulating others to record their memories, the following stand out: *Rodney Cox (1939-1945)*, whose idea this book was, who wrote to over two hundred people who were at the school during the years in question to get a solid body of information together and who has helped to guide the draft in sensible directions; *Geoffrey Mason (1936-1944)* who was Head Boy in his last two years at the school and whose memory is as remarkable as is his generosity with his time; the late *Jack Routh (1940-1944)* who took it upon himself to write to many contemporaries to add their recollections to his; the late *Jean Scragg*, who was from 1944 in charge of all the domestic staff and was the widow of John Scragg, a teacher at the school from 1936 and the Headmaster from 1944 until 1968; *Chris Tod,* curator of Steyning Museum, who is a fount of information and indefatigable in persuading people to record their memories; and *Peter ('Dicky') Wiseman (1940-1946)* who, after a horrified glance at my first attempt at writing this account, not only persuaded me to take a deep breath and start again, but also continued to give constructive comment and advice whenever asked.

Contents

Preface

Like most schools and especially boarding schools, Steyning Grammar School had words used in day-to-day speech which were all its own. 'Slogs' are a case in point. The Steyning Slog was not a reverse sweep for six in cricket, but was a substantial slice of bread which formed the main element of the boarders' breakfast and tea. In my previous book about the school, I used this name in the title, *The Slog Smugglers*. In this book I use the name given to slogs which in the austerity years immediately after the war were sometimes presented late in the meal with no margarine spread on them because the allocation had run out. They were called 'nudes'.

Another word used in the text may need explanation too. 'Librarians' were in later years called 'House prefects'. Above them in the hierarchy were the prefects in the case of librarians and School prefects in the case of House prefects. For both, the powers differed between the two categories.

In this account, each chapter has an introductory section giving background information and setting the scene for what follows. This takes the form of conversations. Some of these actually took place more or less as they appear here, but the majority are imaginary. However, although as gatherings they may be figments of my imagination, their contents are not. The events described did happen as recounted and many of the words used come directly from letters and other communications with Old Boys. So that an unmanageable procession of Old Boys does not parade before the reader, the accounts coming from several different sources have often been compressed and put into a single mouth. It may happen too that a named Old Boy suddenly materialises in a Steyning pub when he and I know all too well that he was living happily in Australia at the time suggested. However, the story-line asks for his account to be given in the first person rather than second-hand. In some instances, where there is disagreement between accounts, or where opinions vary, these differences are aired as arguments or contradictions in the conversations.

Therefore, although I have done my best to write something readable, I have also done what I can to give accurate information about what went on at the school just before, during and just after the Second World War. The main hazard in using the material on which I have drawn is that much of it was recorded some fifty or sixty years later by those who were there at the time. Even so, a good deal has been checked and confirmed by other accounts, by contemporary diaries, by the School Magazines, or by Press articles.

I hope that I have done justice to those who so kindly sent their recollections to Rodney Cox and myself and I am sorry if I have implied in the text more – or less – than they meant.

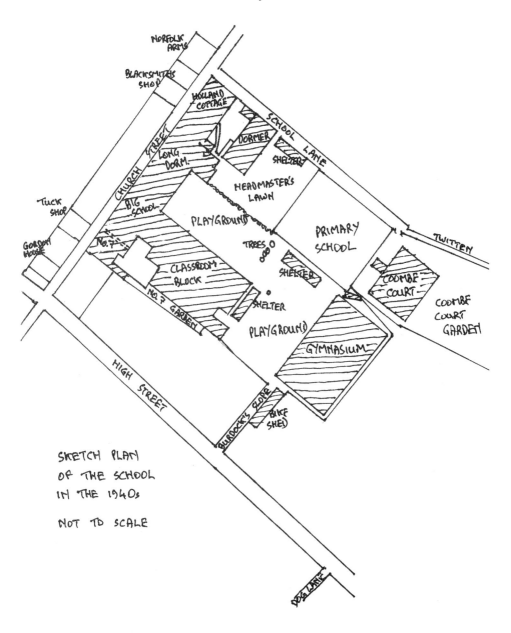

SKETCH PLAN
OF THE SCHOOL
IN THE 1940s

NOT TO SCALE

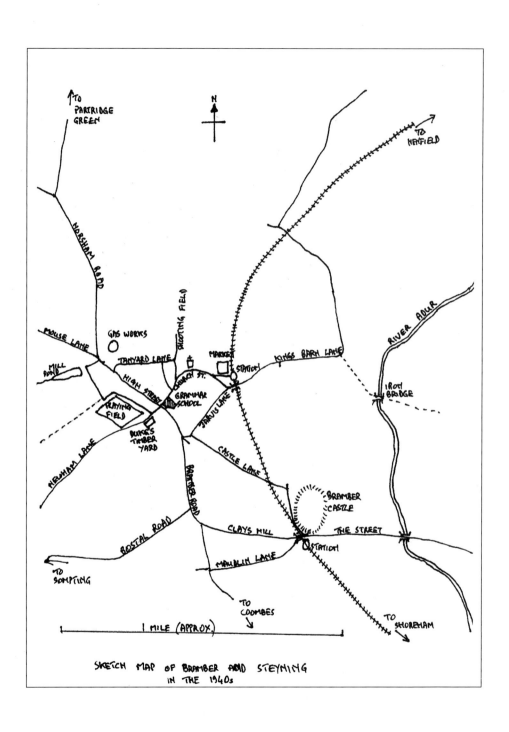

SKETCH MAP OF BRAMBER AND STEYNING
IN THE 1940s

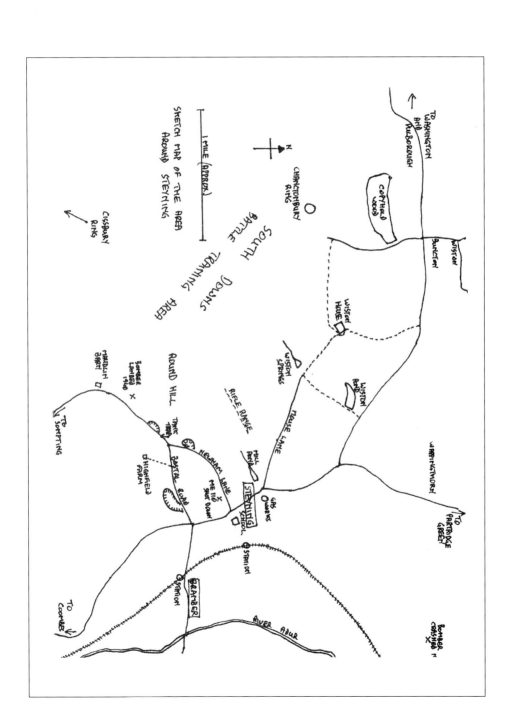

SKETCH MAP OF THE AREA
AROUND STEYNING

1 MILE (APPROX.)

N

CHANCTONBURY RING

CISSBURY RING

SOUTH DOWNS
BATTLE TRAINING AREA

COPYHOLD WOOD

TO WASHINGTON AND PULBOROUGH

WISTON

BURTON

WISTON HOUSE

WISTON POND

WISTON SPRINGS

ROUND HILL

MOUNDAIN BARN

STORAGE LAMBS 1940

HOUSE LANE

RIFLE RANGE

MILL POOL

TANK TRAPS

NEWHAM LANE

POSTAL ROAD

PRE 116 SHOT DOWN

HIGHFIELD FARM

WARMINGHURST

TO PARTRIDGE GREEN

BOTTLEY CRASHED
X

STEYNING SCHOOL

GAS WORKS

STATION

STATION

BRAMBER

RIVER ADUR

TO SOMPTING

TO COOMBES

CHAPTER 1

A storm gathers

THE South Coast of England is no stranger to enemy raids, or even to all-out invasion. Before Julius Caesar rolled ashore in 54 BC and after Duke William's arrival in 1066, Vikings, Angles, Saxons, the Irish, Dutch, French, Spanish and even Moorish slavers, raided sporadically. Then in the late 1930s, another invasion threatened south coast settlements. Rumours of war rumbled around like an approaching thunder storm and there was darkness over Germany.

We look here at how a small grammar school in Sussex coped during the Second World War; at how real threats to the national way of life were treated by schoolboys as a kind of football match; at the relative importance – and imminence – of double Latin with your prep not done, as against that of the future loss of Empire; the shattering impact of the death of one boy in a tragic accident on the playing field, when hundreds died daily, little remarked on by the boys. *'Keep Calm and Carry On'* is a slogan which seems to have been embedded in the psyche of the boys at birth.

About half way between the Sussex seaside resorts of Brighton and Worthing, the River Adur meets the sea in the small commercial harbour at Shoreham. If you walk inland a short way to stand on one of the bridges across the river and look north, the rolling ridge of the South Downs is broken by the broad channel worn by the water through the chalk hills over the centuries. The hills to the right are disfigured by the quarries and derelict buildings of Beeding Cement Works. To the left, Lancing College's lofty chapel makes a more delicate, but hardly less incongruous intrusion on the rounded curves of the Downs. Running alongside the river is the remnant of the track of the Shoreham to Horsham branch railway line, closed in 1966.

The Adur itself is well domesticated, ebbing and flowing sluggishly with the tides over a muddy bed between levées and only occasionally shows now that it was once wild by flooding the fields and any houses rash enough to have intruded on to its plain. It was not always like this and salt-marsh marched alongside the river estuary from the coast for several miles inland. From Norman times and throughout the Middle Ages, this channel through the Downs was guarded by Bramber Castle. This stood at the west edge of the plain and north of the Downs themselves. It would have been seen at once by any traveller coming inland from the coast. Hiding from view, round the corner to the west and nestling at the foot of the hills is the small town of Steyning. Even before Bramber Castle was built, Steyning had some importance. Ships could follow the river estuary inland to a small port just north of the town where cargo could be discharged on to smaller craft to take goods further inland by water, or on to carts to be taken mainly east or west. In those directions roads were passable all year round where they ran along the grain of the Greensands or climbed the 600 feet to the top of the Downs. To travel north, roads crossed heavy clays making winter journeys almost impossible.

At about the same time that Bramber Castle was built, the minster church of St Andrew's (rededicated in 2009 to St Andrew and St Cuthman), linked with its mother abbey of Fécamp, was constructed in Steyning, with the masonry blocks for both being transported there by water. St Andrew's probably replaced a Saxon church which, according to legend, was built by St Cuthman when a sign from God (the wheelbarrow in which he was conveying his mother from the West Country broke here!) suggested to him that Steyning was where he should settle and build a church. St Cuthman seemed to believe in a direct and muscular Christianity, cursing the labourers who laughed when the barrow collapsed and saying that from that time no crops would flourish in the field they were mowing. Part of that field now holds a grammar school boarding house, the rest being divided between a car park and a children's play area, so perhaps an element of the curse remains! Be that as it may, a magnificent set of Norman buildings was put up across the road, if the fragment which remains is anything to go by. Steyning became and remained a fairly important place, if somewhat tenuously so, until the Industrial Revolution. As the years rolled by, the harbour fell into disuse when the estuary silted up in the 14th century; the castle and the minster church decayed; and the dissolution of the monasteries further diminished the place of the church in the community of Steyning. It had become, in effect, a sleepy little market village by the time Drake chased the Spanish Armada up the Channel in 1588. For all that, it clung to pretensions of civic grandeur.

It was here though, in 1614, that wealthy local businessman and Alderman of the city of Chichester, William Holland, decided, as was the fashion of the time, to endow a grammar school to replace the licensed school, which he in fact was probably already paying for. The school was for not more than 50 boys and the income from various local properties was placed at the school's disposal. The school building and Headmaster's house was the former Brotherhood Hall in Church Street, the Brothers having been 'dissolved', as it were. Land immediately associated with the buildings was included in the gift and was expected to be used to help feed the Headmaster and the pupils either by its produce directly, or by income generated from it. The Headmaster also gained income from fees and especially from those charged for boarding. The purpose of the school was to make boys sufficiently literate and numerate to gain entry to public schools; to be equipped with some of the skills which employers looked for; to go on to university; or, the highest goal of schools, to enter the Church. Not a lot changes here as time passes, although there is less prestige these days in going into the Ministry. Discipline was strict and to add insult to injury, each scholar had to pay a penny each quarter towards the provision of 'Brooms and Rods'

Over the next 200 years, the school had mixed fortunes. Occasionally there was a blaze of enthusiasm, but for much of the time the embers glowed but dully in the grate and sometimes nearly went out. After one particularly awful episode, the Headmaster was forced out by the Trustees who, on the grounds that there were so few scholars in the school, decreed that he should have a back-dated pay decrease of 67%, but took with him the key, having locked everything up. In order to get access to inspect the premises, the Trustees had to apply to the Bishop of Chichester for permission to break the lock and replace it with a new one! After this, however, a vigorous North Countryman, George Airey, was appointed in 1839 and he set about him with gusto to get the place up and running and getting it a good reputation. He did precisely this, but when he died the buildings were in such a poor state that the Trustees decided to close the school for the six years 1877-1883, so that repairs and improvements could be made. Although this broke the school's continuity, George Airey's tenure marks the beginning of the grammar school of today. Without him, only ashes might have remained in the grate.

George Airey began a tradition which subsequent Headmasters kept up to various degrees, none more so than John Scragg whose headship ran from 1944 and was the last before the old grammar school became a part of the comprehensive school set up in 1968. Airey's tradition was to help run Steyning itself, which was then very much a rural town with close links with its agricultural surroundings and with a population of around 1500. George Airey teamed up with another vigorous outsider, George Breach, a businessman who owned the tannery. Quite apart from anything else, they campaigned, successfully in the end, to see the Shoreham to Horsham branch railway line constructed and opened in 1861. To achieve this, they had first to revive the fortunes of the town sufficiently for the shareholders in the railway company to see it a worthwhile investment. Its arrival in a way restored Steyning's importance as the transportation hub which the ancient harbour had made it. In particular, it brought fresh life to the livestock markets of the town, transferred after the arrival of the railway from the High Street to fields close to the railway station, and encouraged new businesses on the back of quick and cheap rail transport of materials in and products out. Town and Gown came together here in ways perhaps not envisaged by William Holland, although, as a businessman himself, one cannot but think he would have approved!

The immediate post-Airey repairs to the Church Street buildings, were followed in the early 1900s by the addition of new classrooms and further extensions to the old buildings. Then in the mid-1930s came some major extensions to the school, with more classrooms being added and an Assembly Hall/Gymnasium built. All these works eroded the land originally intended for the Headmaster's use and that available to the boys as a playground.

The picture painted so far gives little feel for the landscape enjoyed and endured by the schoolboys of the late 1930s and 1940s. A bored scholar, looking out of a south-facing classroom window would have seen Steyning Round Hill curving up virtually from sea-level to nearly 600 feet at its summit and from it the whale-backs of the Downs, here mostly clothed in woodland on their steep north-facing slopes, running away to Chanctonbury Ring, three miles to the west. Hidden in these woods are many small chalk pits of some antiquity, but one still active in the 1930s sat on the Round Hill alongside the Bostal Road from Steyning to Sompting across the Downs and another lay off Newham Lane which runs from Steyning to join the Bostal on the Round Hill. The lime kilns in huge pit alongside the Bostal Road just outside the town had closed in 1902. The summit of the Downs and the dip slopes running down to the coastal plain, were mainly grasslands created over the years by intensive grazing of sheep.

If you climb the Round Hill, the view to the north is across quite heavily wooded clay vales with farmlands tucked into them. The main area of open land is the Adur flood plain, curving to the right towards the village of Henfield just north of which the spire of Cowfold Monastery appears. In the far distance, the dim outline can be seen of the Black Down hills of the Lower Greensands beyond Horsham, which hide any glimpse of the North Downs.

In Steyning itself, the main thoroughfare was the A283 which runs roughly on the east/west axis favoured by roads in this area so as to avoid the sticky clays of the Weald. Through the town, as the High Street, this road runs roughly north-west to south-east. Picturesque Church Street, containing the old Brotherhood Hall, joins the High Street about three quarters of the way along it from the Horsham end and opposite this junction is Sheep Pen Lane, giving into Newham Lane which runs up to the Round Hill. At the west end of the High Street, the main road veers to the right, passing Penn's House, once a Quakers Meeting House, where in 1678 William Penn, after whom Pennsylvania is named, came to preach and where Grammar School boarders of the late 1940s got into hot water by blanking out all but one upright in the second letter 'N' of the name. At this corner, Mouse Lane runs straight ahead, leading to Wiston Park, Wiston Pond and Chanctonbury along the foot of the Downs. Mouse Lane is on the Upper Greensand which tends to throw out springs where the overlying Chalk meets it. One such wells up more or less level with the junction of Mouse Lane with the High Street, but a quarter of a mile back towards the Downs. This feeds a mill pond and from thence runs under the High Street and alongside Tanyard Lane where its water was abstracted for use in George Breach's tannery. The tannery closed at the end of 1941, somewhat to the relief of those who did not work there, because of the smell from it which pervaded the town! It is interesting to see that the high quality water found in Steyning's wells and streams, together with the drainage towards the Adur which would flush away the risk of sewage-borne diseases such as cholera, are featured in the School's Prospectus of the 1920s. Even into the 1930s, one of the jobs boarders had to do was pump water up from the school wells into the slate tanks which held it for day-to-day use.

The town has grown and changed in many ways since the 1930s/1940s, but the central core and many of its surroundings, remain instantly recognisable to Old Boys of the Grammar School from those years. Walking about here awakes long-dormant memories of school days; most are pleasant, since the passage of time seems to add to the pleasures whilst eroding the ills of childhood, but are often poignant as former friends now dead, or old and perhaps infirm, are brought back to mind as cheeky schoolboys.

I have yet to find a better way of getting information about the school during those years than arranging to meet small groups of Old Boys over lunch and a pint of beer, preferably in a Steyning pub. When participants have not seen one another for many years, the get-together may take a few minutes to take off. When it does, it is a question of trying, desperately, to pick up and keep all the gems so carelessly and abundantly scattered around – usually while two or more entirely unrelated conversations are going on!

As I edged my way into The Chequer, I looked around to try to spot the people I had come to see. I had not met any of them before, although we had written to one another, and was concerned that, being a bit late, they might have drifted away or be sitting around as disgruntled individuals in a crowded pub. From a table in a corner came a shout of laughter and arms were being waved around as some anecdote was being told; eyes were sparkling and faces animated in a group of half-a-dozen or so elderly gentlemen. I caught the landlord's attention, got myself a beer and made my way across.

"I think you must be the Grammar School Old Boys I'm looking for," I said, "I am George Barker. Sorry I'm a bit late, but I see you have had no trouble recognising each other!"

"To be honest, I don't think any of us would have looked twice at the others had we passed in the street," said one, "After all some of us last met over sixty years back and we looked rather different then! Soon got chatting though – as you see – once we sorted out who we all were. Anyway, Barker, it was good of you to arrange all of this, but how can we help? The old memory is failing a bit here I'm afraid!"

"Well, it sounded from the bar as though someone had remembered **something!** In any case, I have a few School Photos which might jog your minds. Look at this one from 1935. There should be a few familiar faces here!"

The group reshuffled to get a good view and the chatter began. There was a squall of Oh my God! What a lot of scruffs! What's his name? I know the face but can't put a name to it. He gave me six whacks for nothing at all! Then one voice rose above the rest,

"I never liked Bolton as a Headmaster you know, although he did see the building programme through. He looked down on us scholarship boys and his wife was a real snoop and would prowl round the school reporting anything she didn't like and getting boys punished."

"I'm with you over Mrs B, she was a nosey old thing. Did you know that her father was James Elroy Flecker, the poet, and her brother, Oswald, was Headmaster of Christ's Hospital? I expect that she thought that she ought to be a Headmaster too!"

"She certainly acted like one!"

"What was that you were saying about scholarship boys?" I interrupted, "Why would he look down on them? I don't quite understand."

"Ah, yes. In the early 30s, the Powers That Be laid down that Steyning should take as day boys anyone who had passed a scholarship exam. I think that the first, from Henfield at least, was Jack Lewery in 1935. The trouble was that the staff resented having to teach working class yobs and the fee-paying boys seemed to think we were a lower class of being – anyway, that is what it felt like. Bolton made no secret that he felt that university was no place to go to for people from a working class background and when you had got to the school through academic achievement, it went down like a lead balloon to know your HM would far prefer to see a 'posh' boy go on to university than someone like yourself, no matter how dense the 'posh' boy or how bright you were."

"That attitude was a new departure! I remember Charlie Rice complaining of the same thing, but saying too that Attie, the HM before Bolton, was quite the opposite and encouraged anyone with the ability and interest in academia to try for university. He would give special coaching too."

"The 'them and us' attitude to us scholarship boys lasted well after war broke out, you know. I hated one master – can't remember his name, but it doesn't matter – whose idea of humour was in class to pick on one of us who had a Sussex accent and say 'Arr now, do eeh tell us what eeh do fink on im!'. Cheap and nasty, like him. It only changed when the war got serious and Old Boys of all kinds visited the school in uniforms of all kinds too. It drove home the point that we are all the same under the skin – and that bullets don't stop to ask about your accent."

"Trouble was that standard English was the thing. Boys were taught to speak BBC English as part of their educational programme. It was to help you get on in life. Look at poor Wilfred Pickles being taken off reading the news because the public didn't like his Yorkshire accent!"

"I had a friend who was choirmaster at an East End church who made me laugh when he said that most of the choir singing 'Praise Him for His grace and favour' sounded like 'Prize 'im for 'is grice and fiver', but three rather posher ladies sang, shrilly above the rest 'Preeze Him for His grease and fever'. He said that he could have got them all to use standard English, but felt that would be a waste of time because the congregation would immediately put the hymn firmly back on to the road to Stepney!"

"That would not have deterred Mr Barnes!"

"Yes, yes. I didn't mind the Barn Owl dragging you out in front of the class to say 'How now brown cow', or 'Aristotle, Aristotle make haste with the bottle' – and hark to my crystal clear standard English speech now – but that was different to the sneering mockery of this master mimicking you."

"Come on, now! Not all the staff were like that. Razzo Ross, Beef Bennett or the Barn Owl weren't."

"God! Do you remember the Barn Owl playing football! That **was** a shock!"

There was a gale of laughter, so I asked what had happened. It seems that Mr Barnes, who taught classics, history and maths from 1934 until 1939, was a pleasant though quiet and studious man and though liked by most of the boys, was not especially respected by them. He had finicky mannerisms too, like flicking imaginary dust off a chair before sitting on it. There had been astonishment shortly after he came when he was selected to play at centre forward for the school in its annual match against the Town's junior team. No-one could imagine this gentle scholar making any contribution on a football field. Boys did notice – and mock – the fancy football stockings he had dug out from somewhere. Once the game began, the ball soon arrived at the Barn Owl's feet. He promptly set sail for the opposition's goal, shimmering past the entire defence and placing the ball into the net. So far as the spectators were concerned, this had been some glorious fluke and was cheered accordingly. However, the dose was repeated several times and everyone had to admit that, when it came to football, he was something special. Grinning members of the staff who were in the know, then revealed that the Barn Owl had played soccer for Oxford University. His status with the boys rose and, as someone remarked, people began to pay far greater attention to Latin lessons than they had done. He turned out to be a stylish batsman at cricket too, which added to the respect then given to him.

I noticed one of the company looking very thoughtful after that and offered the traditional 'penny for them'.

"I was just thinking how hard it was for people who were no good at games, but were bright. The Barn Owl was brainy, but only got respect when he turned out to be a football wizard. What about boys like Percy Hammond, or old Harris amongst the staff who were clever, but useless at sports?"

"Percy, I do know, hated his time here, but he had other disadvantages too, being a German Jew and a refugee. He and his young brother changed their name from Hamberg while they were at school, I remember. I know that this ought to have brought sympathy and perhaps it did, but there was a definite undercurrent of anti-Jewish feeling."

"I can't agree with you there! I saw absolutely no sign of racial prejudice of that sort at the school."

"There was certainly a fair degree of anti-Jewish feeling in the country at large."

"I'll go along with you there, especially after the war, but I am positive that it didn't extend to the boys in the school in the late 1930s."

"Anyway, Percy was really bright and that was another problem. He knew more than half the staff did and the maths master who taught him in the 6th Form, Bowman, hadn't a clue what to do with him. He got a scholarship to Cambridge, although the Bow told him it wasn't worth his trying and that at a time when we were virtually given a half day's holiday when anyone passed their School Certificate! Went on to become a professor at Southampton University."

"Good for him! But most of the other refugees seemed to fit in pretty well. The Hambergs came late on – 1939, perhaps – along with Rosenthal, Simion, and Rainer, but there were ones more or less contemporaries of mine, who came around 1936 – Fritz Frenckel, Hans Hillelson, and Arthur Levi. They settled in OK and that was when the Riedels were boarders too."

"They were real pro-Hitler and pro-Nazis characters! Pretty sure of themselves, but nice enough lads. Very fit and 'Hitler Youth-ish'. They had a bedroom to themselves in Dormer, decorated with pictures of Hitler. Must have been a bit of a shock having fled from the Nazis on the continent to find the Riedels waiting to greet you at school! There was no trouble though, perhaps neither side really understood what was going on and just mucked in together."

"In fact, Frenckel told me that the Riedels were related to him and that it was because of that he was sent to Steyning. In his first few weeks at the school he got pretty lonely because he had yet to conquer the English language and crept out of his dormitory to go to talk with them. He got caught and was given three whacks, which he still thinks was a bit unfair!"

"Didn't Frenckel knock the younger Riedel's eye out, or something?"

"Reinhold Riedel got a bad injury to his eye, that's certain, but it was playing conkers in the playground with Knapton. Nothing to do with Frenckel. Reinhold wanted to go into the German Navy and we reckoned his bad eye might make him unfit. I don't know what happened there because they both left in 1938 when war with Germany seemed on the cards. His brother, Gerhard, definitely wanted to join the Luftwaffe and when the bomb fell near the school, some people thought it was Riedel!"

"What do you reckon now?"

"Well, I do know that one of the Riedels did say that when he left he would come back with a bomb and that the juniors thought it a splendid idea to put the place out of action, but kids don't think it all through at that age. It was all a bit of a joke, I think. Anyway, it was an acceptably near miss! It is a school myth, but, in its way, attractive!"

While this had been going on, a couple had gone back to the photo again and were chuckling at some memory of Mr Ross, the French master. Claud Ross had arrived at the school in 1919 and spent the rest of his life associated with the school, hanging on to teach throughout the war and dying only three years after he finally retired in 1946. Everyone, from our oldest Old Boy who had left the school in 1922, to those joining the school in 1945, had tales to tell about Razzo. Although a disciplinarian, he was not just respected, but also liked by the boys who detected in him a genuine interest in what they did and achieved. He was as much a stern, but loved, uncle as a teacher. Rather gaunt and with red, cropped hair, he spoke French with a strong Sussex accent and only French was allowed in his classroom. Even a cry of alarm in English when one of his pupils noticed a low-flying German plane closing rapidly on the window, brought a rebuke! He was a very keen cricketer and in his earlier days, would coach the boys. As he got older, arthritis in his hips and legs crippled him, but he insisted playing in the school v staff match throughout the late 1930s. Being unable to run, when it came to fielding he kept wicket. This brought upon him a nickname, 'The Ancient Mariner', because, like Coleridge's old seaman 'he stoppeth one of three'!

"I'll never forget how he used to clump into Room 7! *'Bonjour mes enfants; asseyez vous donc; ouvrez les fenêtres; ou est le torchon?'* In the summer would follow, *'Si vous voulez ôter la veste, ôtez la toute suite.'* Of course we had made sure that all the windows were shut; that the board rubber was nowhere to be found; and that we all had our jackets on. Thought we were all jolly clever and funny!"

"Was it Pennifold who hid the board rubber on the lampshade over Razzo's desk? As soon as the windows were opened, the shade swung and it fell off, just missing the old boy! Confession time for Pennifold!"

"What about his *'petite baguette magique'*? He never really thrashed you, but you were threatened quite often with *'une danse avec Madame la Baguette'* and were warned that *'toutes les choses feminines sont dangereuses'*. From time to time, it was out to the front, bend over the desk and *'trois coups de baguette'!*"

"Do you know that he sent us out to cut sticks out of the hedgerows for the purpose?"

"Remember when Whitehead broke the *'baguette'* into pieces and arranged them on his desk? He played up beautifully, mourning the loss of his *'pauvre baguette'* before opening his desk, selecting a new stick carefully, drawing it lovingly across his palm and inviting Whitehead out for *'une danse'!* I have no idea how he so unerringly picked on the culprit, but there you are, experienced and good schoolmasters have their methods and their helping spirits."

"The worst thing about him from my point of view was all those French names he gave us. It was fine if you were a Robert or a John, both easily turned into the French equivalents, but if there was no obvious equivalent; if there were too many Roberts or Johns; or even if he simply decided that he wanted a few girls in the class, you got landed with a girl's name. Being called Marguerite when you are an eleven-year-old schoolboy is not welcome!"

"I remember poor old Gerald Miller was Sylvie. He was delivering pamphlets or some such and happened to call at Ross's house. Got the shock of his life when a voice boomed out round the town *'Et c'est tu, Sylvie?'*"

"Most of us ended up speaking French, though. I was fluent myself. Only trouble was that when I got to France, no-one could understand me! Quite a few, especially amongst the refugees who had spoken French from an early age, realised that although Ross's French was not quite that of the *'scole of Stratford atte Bowe'*, it was equally not that of France. He was not happy, either, having his pronunciation questioned by a twelve-year-old who had started French with a Parisian lady, I can tell you that! His grammar was fine."

"He could get really roused at times. Remember the cupboard in Room 7? It was a small one just behind his desk and used for storing the blackboard chalk and board rubber – so long as no-one had, like Pennifold, hidden it. He was working at his desk one day when the door became unlatched, swung open and hit the back of his head. Slightly annoyed and muttering imprecations in French, he pushed the door with the back of his hand to close it and without turning round. After a short pause, the door once again swung open and again hit the back of his head. The French became a tad more heated this time as he pushed it back into position and the class began to sit up and take notice, holding its collective breath as the door once more attacked him from behind. They were not disappointed! A furious Razzo rose to his feet swearing loudly in French, ripped the cupboard from the wall, stumped over to the window and hurled the offending item out to crash into the garden twenty feet below. Although highly amused by the whole incident, this amusement was tinged with apprehension at Razzo's strength and fury."

"I wish I'd seen that! He was usually quite gentle with the boys behind a fierce façade, though, so that apprehension was probably misplaced."

"He had a son at the school, didn't he?"

"That's right. Dick. Look, there he is! Third from the left in the back row of the photo. He was a bright lad too and won a scholarship to Ardingly when he was 13. Think he went on to be a professor at the University of East Anglia. Economics or Political Sciences wasn't it?"

"Come on! No politics! We had more than enough of that in the 1930s! Who wants another drink? Hadn't we better order some lunch too?"

After a comfort stop in proceedings and with assorted lunches and fresh drinks supplied, the conversation, stimulated by a second School Photo, this time from 1937, turned towards the Headmaster, Mr Stuart-Clark, who succeeded Mr Bolton in 1937 and, especially interesting to me, because I had known him myself, to John Scragg who assumed the Headship in 1944.

"Old Stuart-Clark was a bit different to Bolton, wasn't he? His wife was pretty, for a start and he was smart and smooth, with a posh car!"

"I can't say that I really warmed to him myself. He seemed more of an admin. type than a teacher. More concerned with the mechanics of running the place than with us."

17

"I thought him a bit off key. He seemed to have the idea that if knowledge didn't go easily into a boy's head, it could be banged in via his backside. I think in my case, it simply increased my natural resistance to acquiring learning. It certainly did not endear him to me."

"Mrs. Stuart-Clark was all right though. She didn't go on the prowl like Ma Bolton, thank God. She used to invite first-year boarders in small groups to afternoon tea. I liked her for that!"

"There speaks a typical boarder – always after food! A clear case of cupboard love!"

"What about Johnny Scragg then?"

"To be honest, he scared me shitless! We called him The Leopard because you never knew when he was going to pounce on you. He just seemed to appear from nowhere when you least expected, or wanted, him. Saturnine and savage – and a Dead-eyed Dick with the cane."

"You didn't take liberties, I grant you, but he really only pretended to be an ogre. He used to come into Big School, leer at us and say 'Test! Anyone getting less than six out of ten gets six of the best!' It never happened, of course."

"Not everyone got away that lightly, although I remember him letting Keith Main off when he fired a blank-cartridge starting pistol in his jacket pocket by accident in the middle of the lesson. There was this hell of a bang; Scraggy and the rest of us jumped out of our skins; Main sat there looking terrified, with a cloud of smoke above him and a bloody great hole in his jacket pocket, wishing he had never been born. That look of terror probably saved him. Scraggy just confiscated the pistol and it was used for starting races on Sports Day."

"Your mention of terror reminds me how really scared I was when John Scragg appeared in Long Dorm after lights-out on my first day at the school with an African ritual mask on. He then told us that St Cuthman's ghost would sometimes appear under the beam above my bed, but said that it never did on the first day of term. Most of the others took it as a joke, but I was petrified."

"Someone told me he had been in Africa and got malaria, which was why he was out of sorts from time to time, but I don't know whether that was true."

"I can help you there," I interposed, "He and Arthur Bolton were both in what was then the Gold Coast as foundation staff for the new Achimota College in Accra. Bolton came back and took up the Headship here, but John Scragg got interested in the work of the Government Anthropologist, retrained in anthropology, and went to work up-country, where he did indeed contract malaria. When that work was wound up, he returned to England and Bolton asked him to come to help out at Steyning on a temporary basis. He was writing a book with another of the foundation staff of Achimota, but that was about finished. It is a grammar called *Common Errors in Gold Coast English* and was still in use in Ghana not long ago and was way ahead of its time when written. Anyway he came to Steyning. His post was subsequently made permanent and he got a ground-floor flat in Dormer, but in his first spell as a stop-gap he had the corner cubicle in Long Dorm, which must have been pretty awful for all concerned! I have been told tales of him treating himself for a malaria attack using quinine in the form of tonic water in combination with the usual liquid traditional to tonic water and, being unable to get to sleep, playing a couple of records throughout the night, singing along and using a pencil on the bottles as a percussion accompaniment! He did still get attacks of malaria certainly into the 1950s when I was at school."

"I never knew that he was into anthropology, but he was certainly very keen on local history and things like that. We used to go on long walks on the downs, fossicking in the mole-hills for bits of pottery and flints which we would take back to him. We had to pin-point on a map where we had found them. He would take a few of us at a time out in his car too to look at places like Chichester Cathedral. So he could be friendly, but he was definitely intimidating! That book, which I didn't know about, helps explain why he could get amongst us so easily over poor grammar! It is a thought typical of the Empire days, that when we forced the natives to speak English as a second language, we expected them to damned well speak the King's English and not evolve an English of their own. Didn't really work, did it?"

"The evidence would seem to be against it. I did cherish one of the book's opening remarks that it set out rules to prevent recurrence of errors and that 'Nothing that its rules allow can be wrong.' This reflects the absolute certainty of the John Scragg edicts which I recall!"

"You have read the thing? You must be a masochist!"

"Well, not to say 'read', but I have dipped into it. It is quite interesting actually, but not light reading, I'll grant you."

"There was a good story about John Scragg when he became Headmaster in 1944. Apparently the Governors had given him Thursday afternoon off, but wanted him to teach the first period after lunch. Not wanting to waste any of his precious time off, he appeared in Big School dressed in cricket whites and carrying his bat. This he placed on the master's table and wrote 'Test' on the board. Anyone doing badly in the test was yanked out and asked to bend over. 'I need to practice my late cut' or whatever. In the first such period after the cricket season had ended, he marched into Big School, dressed for shooting and carrying his twelve-bore, which he placed on the table and wrote 'Test' on the board. There was a good deal of panic in the ranks!"

"Typical! Pretending to be the ogre again! But he could be generous too."

"'Bumps' Bristow told me that Scraggy used to lend him his bike in the afternoons, but when he found that Bumps had been using it to see a girl he went ballistic. Then he fell flat on his back skating on Wiston Pond and Bumps creased up laughing, so that was the end of the bike for another week!"

"Do any of you recall Geoffrey Kitchener?" I asked, "He was a boarder between 1940 and 1946, so would have been a lot junior to many of you. He was a nice guy, with a robust sense of humour and I got to know him quite well in the three years or so before he died. He told me a lot. He had a great pride in the school and respect for John Scragg. In fact he said that there were only two people in the world whom he automatically and willingly called 'Sir': one was his Colonel in the Middlesex Regiment; the other was John Scragg.. He was not the tidiest boy in the school and when he called on the Scraggs unannounced and after they had retired to Partridge Green, he drove up in his open-topped sports car, John glanced up from the rose bed, beamed and said 'Typical Kitchener! Hair all over the place!'"

"Did he tell you about the time when Stuart-Clark had said that anyone caught scrawling graffiti would be expelled and then Kitchener came across a note on the bog wall saying 'Hamberg is a weed and a worm' and wrote under it in red chalk 'We agree' and signed it with the names of all the staff and prefects he could think of? He was caught, literally red-handed, by Dallyn, who was a prefect and was terrified that he was for the chop. S-C just ticked him off saying that this sort of thing could lead to him committing serious forgery when older. He was pretty relieved, but felt that it was a bit rich to say this to an 11-year-old!"

"One thing I will say for Scragg was that he didn't have favourites. Tom Baines was a great teacher and just about everyone liked him, but he did have favourites. I'm afraid I was one and we used to get taken out for strawberries and cream and go rowing on the river. I was a bit worried, but nothing ever happened and who was I to say no to some extra grub!"

"Another case of a boarder's cupboard love! Anybody's for an extra slog!"

"Gertcha!!"

20

"Thompson, the PT bod, had his favourites too and they would go round for tea at his place. As you said about 'Shirty' Baines, I never heard that anything happened. He could be a bit of a sadist though, sitting boys in gym kit on the gym radiators as a punishment. He had to teach Maths and Music too, but he was no specialist in either!"

"I must say that I was a bit anxious when he towelled you down after your shower at the end of gym. You had first to put your hands on his shoulders while he tried to rub the skin off your back and then turn to hang on to the coat hooks while he repeated the dose to the front, but nothing untoward ever happened, I'm pleased to say."

"What I remember best about him was his car. It had the registration letters FMT and we said it stood for 'Free Meals Thompson' because he often stayed to eat school meals!"

"He must have been desperate to do that!"

"I dunno, I **liked** the school meals!"

"Boarders again!!"

"Wasn't Baines wounded in the First World War? We always called him Captain Baines and he couldn't bend one of his knees."

"We were told he had been shot through his knee-cap. It used to stick out like a flag-pole when he used the fire escape pulley from his room over the main entrance during fire drills!"

"The chap who took over as housemaster for the boarders from Baines didn't have favourites, but was very popular. You didn't mess about, but he was never in the John Scragg league as a frightener! Stanley Bayliss Smith."

"SBS was a good one! I've never found anyone with a bad word for him. A brilliant photographer and spent ages getting good ones of birds. We got pulled in to help with his bird-watching studies too."

"If you had to go to see him, you quite often found him developing films in his darkroom. He would always explain what was going on and it was fascinating. I still dabble in photography and print my own because of him."

The conversation drifted on in a desultory way until someone said he must make a move and the rest gathered coats and hats too and said their goodbyes, thanking me profusely for setting up the meeting and promising everyone that they would now keep in touch.

As I left, I heard someone at a nearby table say "It is easy to see that they were comrades in arms. You can always tell old soldiers!" Well, perhaps they were comrades in arms in a sense, but school gives a link between people which military service does not. At school you change from being a child into a man, doing so in the company of others with whom a special bond is forged by sharing this profound metamorphosis.

CHAPTER 2

Running for cover

During the last three years of the 1930s, the political situation in Europe degenerated rapidly. It was obvious to many, if not to all, that war with Germany was a real possibility. In the spring of 1938 Germany annexed Austria and in the autumn laid claim to the German-speaking parts of Czechoslovakia. A round of shuttle diplomacy was begun between Chamberlain and Hitler, culminating in the Munich agreement. In Britain, re-armament was stepped up; plans were made to evacuate London; gas masks were issued; the ARP was mobilised; air raid trenches were dug in open spaces; white lines were painted on kerbs and lamp posts; and, for the first time in peace, conscription into the Armed Services was announced. On 1 September 1939, Germany invaded Poland and on 3 September Chamberlain announced that we were at war with Germany. Between June 1939 and the first week of September three and a half million people were moved from areas thought to be unsafe and Departments, institutions and companies were dispersed from London.

What followed immediately the declaration of war was a mixture of earnest endeavour and farce, particularly in the south east of England which took the brunt of the evacuation of London's children, or, rather, the evacuation of such of London's children whose parents allowed it. Since, because of this, only half the children were evacuated, a mockery was made from the very outset of the ideal that all children should be able to continue their education in safety and without interruption. There could be situations where only half of the children of a school were moved out, leaving half behind. On which group should the teachers concentrate? Sussex in fact received only half of the evacuees expected and those who had worked so hard to find suitable accommodation were disillusioned. One twelve-year-old boy from Ashurst summed up his feelings: *"Everybody in the village had to take evacuees and we waited for days on end for these evacuees to come to the village but..... they never arrived in the village and quite a lot of us were disappointed."* Of those who were evacuated, a fair number very swiftly decided – or their parents decided for them - that life in the country was not for them and went back home. Once the blitz on London began in 1940, there was a sluggish drift back out of the city.

The country had been divided into three categories: those most at risk from attack and which should be evacuated; those to which the threat was not imminent and from which there should be no immediate evacuation; and receiving areas, considered safe for those who had been forced to move. Most of Sussex was a receiving area. The coastal towns were at first seen as low risk areas, but then as invasion became a possibility, in theory at least, there was some evacuation from them of school children whose schools had not themselves already been moved inland for the duration.

Although many of the primary schools in Sussex had to cope with hosting schools which had been evacuated, Steyning Grammar School, being a selective secondary school and with many boys resident in the buildings, was never put under that kind of pressure. It did indeed take a number of evacuees, but many for only a short time. Some pupils who under different circumstances would have been day boys, were taken as boarders to get them away from the bombing raids on the coastal towns. Others were removed by their parents and sent to other schools because Steyning was felt to be too close to the coast for safety should there be an invasion.

The result from the Grammar School's point of view was an unprecedented ebb and flow of boys during the first bit of the war. This probably affected adults far more that the boys concerned, who seem to have accepted the vagaries of adult perceptions and preferences simply as part of life's rich pattern and to have settled down to extract the last ounce of enjoyment from any confusion caused; from any chinks in the armour of staff drafted in to fill gaps; from the opportunities for adventure and mischief thrown up by the conflict itself; by the proximity of soldiers under training and the panoply of war which they bore with them, or, more particularly, that which they left behind them. The only major down side to all of this was experienced by the most senior boys who found themselves comprehensively outbid by the soldiers when competing for the attentions of the local girls. The more junior boys did not suffer from this problem!

There were just the six of us. We had arranged to visit the School to have a look round and see how much things had changed. As is usual on such visits, it seemed as though the buildings had shrunk. Corridors were not so long and classrooms were much smaller than we had remembered!

23

Still, it had been a good expedition, bringing back a lot of memories and had taken long enough for us to accept the offer of a cup of tea with alacrity and gratitude. I thought that at least one of the Old Boys had been an evacuee and that it was a good opportunity to sort out some points which had been puzzling me.

"Rodney, you were an evacuee, weren't you? How many were there at the school? I get the impression from the records that there weren't a lot."

"I don't think that there were. There were the refugees, of course, but they were in a different boat. Some of the evacuees only stayed a short time. The Decent brothers, for example, were only at Steyning for a couple of months before they went back to London. It depends on what you call an evacuee too. There were day boys from places like Shoreham who were moved inland, but who were at the school the whole of the time."

"But you were what I would call a proper evacuee, sent away from London for safety and staying for a good few years."

"That's right in a sense. When war broke out we were staying with my grandparents in Rustington. I remember rushing out to stand on the gate to look out across the sea for the first invaders flying in! Nothing came – most disappointing! I went as a boarder to SGS that term and I expect that it was thought best for my safety, although when I wrote home cheerfully in 1943 about being narrowly missed by a bomb and the High Street being machine-gunned by a Dornier and then some months later about the town being shelled by accident one Sunday, I think that my mother began to think that Ealing was safe by comparison. It is amazing how insensitive we were at that age. It had all been a bit of excitement and so, naturally, it went into our letters home. No thought at all for our parents' feelings! Anyway, it did not stop me going home in the holidays, so it can hardly be seen as a 'proper' evacuation. Dicky Wiseman was another junior boarder in the same boat. His home was in Littlehampton and he went back there in the holidays, although it, like Shoreham, got a regular sprinkling of bombs. Someone like Algy Haughton was a more genuine evacuee who came from Croydon with his family and they lived in Steyning for a couple of years with him coming to the school as a day boy."

"Mine was a genuine evacuation too," observed John Sennitt, "But entirely voluntary on the part of the family. We were not asked to go. We were on holiday in the Lake District and my father decided that it would not be safe to go on living where we were in Hanger Hill – he had a chemist's shop on The Mall in Ealing – and we were to move into a property near Storrington, owned by his sister. No sooner were we established there than war was declared. My father got up each day at 6am to commute into Ealing and returned home at around 9pm. Long hours! I was a day boy, like Algy, but had a bit further to travel"

"At least you got your holiday John!" chipped in another, "We had just gone on holiday to the Isle of Wight the week before war was declared. It was my first proper holiday because we were not that well-off and even then we booked into an old railway carriage, parked, along with others, in a field – self-catering, of course, but my mother preferred it like that! As the rumours of war became stronger, my father, who had experienced the First World War as a warrant officer in the Navy, decided that we must return home at once to Fishersgate in case the military requisitioned all the trains. The bloody war deprived me of my first real holiday and I have not forgiven Hitler for it! However, the war did bring me some benefits, because I was indeed evacuated for a spell. When it was felt that there was a genuine threat of invasion, the Headmaster, Mr Stuart-Clark, devised a scheme whereby those like me, who lived on the coast, would be moved out of the danger zone to stay with pupils who lived inland. I went to Storrington which is only sixteen miles from the coast, so I don't suppose it would have been that much safer there. It was a bit of fun though, but the really important thing was that I learnt to climb trees! The ones in urban Fishersgate were not suitable for climbing, but the Storrington area was full of good trees and as a result of being evacuated I acquired this most useful skill. I suppose I have Hitler to thank for that – but my lost holiday still rankles!"

"I can't think off hand of anyone else who Stuart-Clark organised like that, but some from the coastal areas did come as boarders. Tony Randle lived in Brighton and was bundled off to Steyning as a boarder."

"Others got shoved about more than that! I remember that Tim Ashby said that his mother, sister and he were sent in 1940 to stay with an uncle and aunt in Worcester and were there for about a year. He then went to Steyning as a boarder, although the family home was in Shoreham."

"Some folk did not see Steyning as safe enough. The Leveson's mother took them away and sent them as day boys to a school near West Chiltington where they lived, because she was scared that, if the Germans invaded, she would not be able to get to the boys in Steyning and so preferred them nearby. Jeremy Lawson went to Cornwall in 1940 after a couple of years at the school. Alan and Deryk Jones went one better. They went with their family to Canada and I think came back to Steyning after the war."

"They did," I said, "Alan sent me a letter some time back which gave the details."

"The Barn Owl went to Canada too, didn't he? We heard that he was offered a teaching post there."

"That's right, but I heard he was on the *Athenia* when it was torpedoed and I don't know if he was one of the survivors or not. We never heard so far as I know. I hope he survived. I liked him."

"Its fame of a sort, I suppose, to have your Latin Master sunk in the first ship to be destroyed in the war!"

"I happened to be going through the old School Magazines on our Archive CD," mentioned another, "And noticed a comment in the 1944/45 issue that 'Major RC Barnes, RA, has been doing very hush-hush work in Italy'. If so, he certainly survived – if he was in fact on board. There is nothing I saw which said where he went after the war."

"Good to hear he was OK in 1945. He was a decent master."

Roy Moore continued the main theme. "We lived in Southwick and in March 1941, I was sent away because of the threat of invasion. There were several of us and I had a friend with me for the train journey to Doncaster – quite an adventure! We were billeted with families in Bawtry. We liked it there and enjoyed half-day schooling because of the limited school room. Then, in late August I was told I had to go back to Southwick and attend Steyning Grammar School as a day boy. To hell with any danger, a good schooling was more important!"

"Better a dead scholar than a live dunce, eh!"

"Noel Waine moved to Steyning from Hertford for his health, you know. He told me that his parents were advised to get him closer to the sea and felt that Steyning met the bill. He said that after his mother saw a bomb fall in broad daylight half way between their house and the prep school he was at, that she felt the dangers would not be much greater in Steyning. However, the choice of Steyning was not the result of a risk-assessment, but from a study of brochures from comparable schools."

"I know that one boy came to us from London quite late on in the war really, but I suppose that the buzz-bombs and continuing air raids were an incentive here! Moules came in 1943 and stayed three years. We called him 'The Cockney Kid' and I don't think he liked it, or us, a lot."

"Don't blame him!"

"I remember that one boy was moved from Steyning closer to London! That was not from choice, though."

"Who was that?"

"Ken Hiscock. They had a farm on the Downs by the Steyning Bowl. It was called Annington Hill Barn and was really a cottage close to agricultural buildings. A track ran from it up to the Bostal Road. Don't you remember that he sometimes rode a horse the couple of miles or so to Steyning, left it to be re-shod at the blacksmiths opposite the school and collected it after school to ride it back? Anyway, at one point about eighty soldiers turned up and took over all the farm buildings and, because the farm had a phone, half the house too. Then two days later, decided that they were at the wrong farm and disappeared in the night taking with them everything which wasn't bolted down! It was a taste of things to come. The land was requisitioned in 1941, at very short notice, as part of the battle training area and they were kicked out. The land had belonged to the Passmores and Mr Hiscock was a tenant. He was lucky and ended up as manager of a dairy farm near Guildford."

"Must be rotten to be turfed out like that, especially after you had put a lot of work in on the land."

"Yes, Ken said that as they left, the tanks were bashing over the fences his father had maintained so well. I wouldn't blame them for feeling bitter, war or no war."

"The barns are still there, but their cottage was demolished and never rebuilt."

"For some kids, you know, it must have been quite a strain, swapping schools so much. Roddy Stevens told me he was evacuated from Bognor to Cornwall with his prep school in 1940, and then came into Form 1 at Steyning in 1942 when the threat of invasion receded. Two years later he was taken away because we dropped Latin which was essential for School Cert and entry to university; went to another prep school for cramming for Common Entrance; and then got a scholarship to Leys School in Cambridge. Seemed to have done him no harm though."

"It wasn't just the boys who were shifted about. The staff ebbed and flowed too."

"Some of the ebb was due to us I reckon. Some were hopeless at keeping order. After having a frightener like Bill Lewis for Maths, you were liable to let off a bit of steam when Bowman replaced him when he was called up. Poor old Harris was reduced to tears in Latin once when the form was really round his neck and had let the biology lesson's frogs out round the classroom. He left shortly afterwards. He came in 1940/41 and only lasted until 1941/42. Come to think of it, there was a gap of a year between him leaving and Padden coming to teach Latin amongst other things and that must have been why Roddy Stevens left! I don't know how old Charlie Chaplin survived. He was still teaching well after the war ended. We had him for History and English and it was a riot – never as bad as Larynx Harris's classes, but pretty wild all the same."

"I was there when Charlie really lost it. We'd all been winding him up, you know, one boy humming and then another in a different part of the class, and Charlie going 'There's a boy hummmmming! We can't have hummmmming!'. Anyway, he thought that Woolf was the ringleader and came storming down the class and fetched him a clip round the ear, good and hearty. Woolf was over six foot and Charlie was knee high to a grasshopper. Woolf slowly unwound himself, towering over Charlie and said, menacingly, 'Do that **again**, sir!' Charlie, still beside himself with rage, shouted 'All right, I will!' and fetched him another resounding blow. Collapse of Woolf and the class was very well behaved after that – well, for a couple of days anyway."

"Woolf got his own back, of course! Geoffrey Kitchener, now dead, alas, told me about the time Charlie took boarders' evening prayers. It was just a couple of prayers – you know, 'Our Father…' and 'Lighten our darkness…' – plus a hymn. Thing was, if you remember, that Charlie was an agnostic or something, and in Assembly just stood there not singing or saying 'Amen' or anything. Normally, he refused to take evening prayers, but this time there was just no-one else to do so. Had he been wise, he would have asked the Holland House Captain to do the honours and all would have been well. He underlined his lack of wisdom by asking Kitchener to lend him a prayer book and to mark a suitable prayer for him. Having armed one of his leading tormentors with a mouth-watering array of possibilities for mischief, he found that Peter Woolf, who was an excellent pianist and good enough an organist to play in church, was to play the hymn and asked him to select one. Prep ended and Charlie mounted the Big School rostrum, giving out the hymn number. Woolf had chosen 'For All the Saints Who from Their Labours Rest', which goes on for ever as it is. He had also improvised a splendid introduction which went on for about as long as the hymn, full of 'f's and 'ff's , crashing chords and riffles up and down the keyboard. After a minute or so Charlie's voice rose above the din 'For God's sake get on with it Woolf!' Eventually, the boarders' voices gave out and Charlie prepared to read Kitchener's prayer, which he now found was the one for the Churching of Women after child-birth! Not the obvious one for a boys' boarding House. Realising this, he extemporised along the following lines: ' Um, er…Dear God, we thank

Thee for….that boy, stop talking….we, er, bless Thee for all Thy, er, blessings…. there is somebody hummmming!......we pray for peace and, er, um, peace…..Hart, take a hundred lines….. O Christ!…. O God…. Kitchener! Detention!.....er, O Lord, Amen.'"

"Charlie was liked as well as ragged a lot. If you gave him a chance he was a good teacher and he had written what we thought then were a couple of pretty steamy novels about ancient Rome. One got into the library for a short time and you simply had to let it open by itself to find the best bits. I recall that *The Pagan City,* or was it his other one, *The Lust for Power,* began 'Julia cast her last shred of clothing from her and stumbled on over the burning sand.' Then it disappeared. I think that Charlie cottoned on after some embarrassing questions from his English classes! His writing did bring him a bit of respect, but that did not stop explosive chemicals being spread 'where ere he walked'; an alarm clock timed to go off in mid-period being hidden under the Big School dais; the master's table being put right on the edge of the Big School dais so that it would fall off as soon as he touched it; or the class in Room 4 lifting the desks off the floor by skilful use of hands and legs and indulging in synchronised swaying and circling of furniture while Charlie went red, stuttered and bubbled!"

"Chris Passmore – he is still farming at Coombes, by the way – told me that when he was a boarder, Charlie invited him and another boy, Taylor, to tea one Sunday at his house in Roman Road. They were pretty surprised, but at the appointed time, two rather giggly schoolboys made their way there and were made most welcome by Charlie and his wife, who was as short and stout as Charlie. They had a superb tea with freshly baked scones, cream, strawberry jam and fruit and sponge cakes, all very different to the slogs and marge at school! This treat evidently stuck, because when Charlie came to leave in 1947 to take up another teaching post, Passmore and Taylor went to say goodbye to him, knocked on the staffroom door and told him that they had come to say goodbye. He shook them warmly by the hand and there were tears in his eyes."

"Larynx Harris was absolutely useless with the lower school, but I know that Geoffrey Goatcher found him a good and helpful teacher in the 6th Form. In fact he says the Harris was the only member of staff to take any real interest in his doings and was a major factor in getting him to university. John Colebrook, on the other hand, usually a pleasant and polite young man, who later became the respected Deputy Head of a well-known school in Australia, couldn't get on with him at all and once threw his textbook on to the top of the book cupboard and stormed out of Latin, shutting the classroom on the door, as it were, as he left!"

"A bit risky that in Larynx's class! They would put black shoe polish on the door knob, because, when things got out of hand, he would go to the door and hold on to the knob shouting that he was going to fetch the headmaster!"

"The Arts were not the only classes to suffer! How about Major Child in Science classes. He was all of sixty when he came to us in 1941 and seemed to have forgotten anything he ever knew. Just made you copy chunks out of the textbook. We spent about a term boiling water and letting it cool down, taking its temperature at intervals. I still don't know why! The alternative was endless titrations in chemistry. He called everyone 'Abominable Boy' and drank water out of lab beakers. *'The good old Major's dead/ We'll see his face no more/ For what he thought was H_2O/ Was H_2SO_4.'*"

"He always played with a glass flask. It was a kind of nervous habit. One day David Roe heated it up with a Bunsen burner before he came in. He picked it up as usual and the thing went several feet into the air as it burnt him. We got a well-earned detention for that – but it was worth it and a good laugh at the time."

"I remember him clumping down the corridor, jangling a bunch of keys. He had a marvellous memory, you know. I had been in Africa and in 1968 came back on furlough and was walking up East Street in Shoreham when, to my amazement, I saw him coming towards me. I was quite surprised and said 'Major Child!' He stood, gazed at me and then shut his eyes - probably hoped that I was a nightmare and would vanish! Opening them again, he beamed and said, 'Bennett! You were going into the church. How are you?' It had been over twenty years since he last saw me. Incredible!"

"Buff Bennett was the other science teacher, wasn't he? I must say I didn't find him particularly inspiring, but he did know his stuff."

"He was a kindly old chap at heart. One day I skipped the junior walk, which he was taking, but then got bored of hiding in the Art Room and dreamt up a wheeze. I would load one of the Art Room windows with water – if you recall, they opened on a centre hinge and so could lie horizontally – and give one of my friends a bath when he passed below as the walk came back up Burdock's Slope and into the playground. All went as planned, I listened for footsteps and tipped the window up. There was an adult yell from below and there was Buff glaring up. Well, I took to my heels along Upper Corridor, trying to get to the Big School landing and mingle with the rest. Buff beat me to it, collared me and took me to the staff room. Here he dug out a cane and indicated the position. I heard the swish of the cane and then…..nothing! 'Stand up Brown,' he said, 'This is your lucky day – you missed and so did I.'"

"Typical of the man! Benevolence in tweeds!"

"His old mother was kind too in her way. When they were in charge of Coombe Court, she kept a record of the boys' birthdays and would bake a cake for them. Quite a sacrifice with the rationing in force."

"Do you remember how she would tip her chamber pot out of a top window to save her carrying it down the stairs? It did the bush underneath no good at all – and we made damned sure that the dormitory window below was closed once we realised what was going on!"

"Happy days!"

"We have probably outstayed our welcome here you know, but there is just one thing I **must** do before we go – ring the School Bell! It is still there in the playground, but they use electric bells these days to signal the end of lessons and all the things that old bell used to control."

We wandered out into the playground where the tallest was deputed to do the deed. As the nostalgic sound rang out, a lady caretaker came out of the door at the bottom of the stairs up to Big School.

"You Old Boys are all the same when you come back to visit. No matter how ancient you are, you turn back into fourteen-year-olds! As soon as I hear that bell being rung after school, I say to myself 'it's one of those Old Boys again' and it always is."

"Ah! But you can't make us go and stand outside the Headmaster's study for a caning any more."

"If only!! It would do some of our present crop a world of good – not that they are a bad lot of kids on the whole"

CHAPTER 3

Feeding the appetites

From the lessons learnt in the First World War, it was clear that arrangements had to be made to be sure that such food and other commodities as were necessary were shared equitably. Also, that attention be diverted from manufacturing luxury goods to making basic necessities, for example fine bone china ceased production and was replaced by the thick pottery cups, plates and similar crockery which still lurk in many kitchen cupboards, including my own! The major diversion of effort went, of course, into manufacturing armaments. Although the lack of crockery and the abundance of ordnance lost or left behind by our military, or donated from on high by the enemy, gave the boys opportunities for enjoyment, food was a major concern to a school full of active and growing children. It was also a considerable headache for the adults charged with feeding them. This applied to the day boys living at home, but with the boarders it bulked especially large.

During the inter-war period, many of the poorer families had a diet deficient in proteins and vitamins. This led to high incidences of rickets, dental decay, anaemia and TB, with the families of farm workers amongst the worst affected. A study made at the time of the Cuckfield Rural District Council area, which is not that far from Steyning, showed that 33% of the children were undernourished. When rationing was devised, it attempted to go some way to rectifying things.

The other and more obvious problem to be got round was that Britain imported during the 1930s, 92% of its fats, 51% of its meat and bacon, 73% of its sugar, 87% of its flour cereals and high proportions of its consumption of eggs, cheese, vegetables and fruit. It was anticipated, correctly, that these imports, all of which came by sea, would be disrupted in a time of war. The supplies which got through would need to be used carefully. Every effort had to be made to produce in this country a great deal more of the food we eat. However, since many adults were to be engaged in active military service or the manufacture of armaments, there were fewer people to do so. Women and children, including the Steyning schoolboys, helped to fill the gaps.

The actual mechanics of rationing were quite complicated. It was clear that you could not treat the population as a homogenous unit. Although the majority of adults could be, those engaged in hard physical work needed more food than those in less wearing occupations. Then, there were the special dietary needs to be met of pregnant women; of babies and infants; of children; some categories of invalids; vegetarians; and some religious groups. Certain foods were seen as absolutely basic and these were rationed and you expected to get your weekly ration as of right. Others were on 'points' and you could buy what you wanted to – when it happened to be there in the shop – up to the limit of your allocation of points. The points system came in late in 1941 and of particular interest to schoolboys were the personal points for sweets! Points were also needed for clothes and, if you wanted to be really popular, you saved points to give as a present on special occasions. Thanks to bureaucracy, my mother was given such an opportunity when my twin sisters were born in 1945. She got extra points, of course, for both babies, but she also got two sets for herself because the rule was one set of maternity wear per baby, so twins meant two sets of maternity clothes for her! Having, in those years of make-do and mend, all the clothes she had worn previously when producing myself and my younger brother, she had become a clothing points millionaire and was **extremely** popular!

Everyone was registered and issued with a ration book which contained your ration coupons and points for a year. No ration book: no food! You made sure that it, together with your identification card and gas mask, were with you when you took shelter from an air raid! For children between 5 and 18, the ration book was a blue one (RB4) but the allocations were virtually the same as those for civilian adults (RB1, buff) except that children had priority for milk. The actual mechanics of how you then acquired things need not concern us here because this was handled by the adult world – with the jealously guarded exception of sweets. For the boarders, the week's points for sweets were handed over together with the week's pocket money, both usually exchanged for booty in the Tuck Shop across Church Street from the school in a very short span of time. Mrs Stuart-Clark also ran a small tuck shop in the dining hall during school breaks. The sweet ration was initially 8 ounces each month, but thereafter varied between 12 ounces and 1 pound per month; 2 ounces a week at the minimum and 4 ounces at the maximum.

That aside, parents and the school handled all the basics such as food and clothing. Obviously for day boys it was the parents who managed most of this, although there would have been an arrangement with the school over the coupons and points needed to supply lunch where this was wanted. For the boarders, the school held all their ration books during the term, returning them to parents for the holidays. There were distinct advantages in catering for large numbers during rationing and the boarders benefited – although they by no means appreciated this at the time!

So, what were the school caterers faced with, or perhaps more importantly, what did they have to do without? Most things were rationed by weight, but these were varied according to supplies, so that over the course of time the weekly allocation of bacon and ham ranged between 4 and 8 ounces; butter 2-4 ounces (later combined with margarine as a 6 ounce ration, which together with 2 ounces of cooking fat made up your 'fats' ration); sugar 8-16 ounces; cheese 1-8 ounces; tea 2-4 ounces; and preserves 8-32 ounces per four weeks (for most of the time 16 ounces, i.e. 4 ounces per week). To these basics you added items available on points, if and when they became available in the shops. In practice, there were few real shortages in the outlying rural areas of England, Wales and Scotland. In the big cities, on the other hand, it was sometimes very difficult to get even your rations. You were encouraged to supplement your diet with home-grown produce and with any birds, mammals and fish which were palatable and obtainable within the law – well, without breaking the law too blatantly – and with the fruits of the hedgerows. Again, this was all very well in the rural areas, but was much more of a problem in places such as London. There was, of course, a flourishing black market in all parts of the country, especially after the war - other than in Steyning, of course!

Two of the mainstays of school meals were not rationed at any time during the war – bread and potatoes. This accounts for the huge tonnage of slogs consumed by the boarders and although it is not claimed as a record, one boy's diary records consumption of 12 slogs over a fifteen minute period one tea-time and slogs were substantial chunks of bread! After the war, from 1946 until 1948, bread was rationed and this may have had an impact on the bread consumption, but if so, it was scarcely noticed by the boys since it has not been mentioned by any. Potatoes were rationed too when the severe winter of 1947 disrupted transport in the countryside. Potatoes were scarcely less significant than slogs so far as boarders were concerned and cheese and potato pie for tea was something of a treat. It is still a comfort food of mine, although I now add chopped bacon and a topping of grated cheese and a few caraway seeds to the basic mix of sliced onions, potatoes and grated cheese, moistened with milk and baked in the oven for 45 minutes.

It was often said that the local butcher would be seen returning from the market driving two fine beasts to slaughter for the townsfolk, plus one scrawny old hack for the school. There is a plausible thread which can be followed here, because meat was not rationed by weight, but by price. When rationing started for meat in March 1940, you were allocated fresh meat worth 1 shilling and 10 pence per week. In 1941 and again in 1948 the amount was reduced to 1 shilling and the maximum during the years for which rationing lasted was 2 shillings and 2 pence. Unlike most other things, you could not carry your ration over into the following week or back from the next week. If you did not claim it in the week concerned, you lost it. Therefore, in order to cater for the normal need of boys for quantity ahead of quality, the school bought the largest quantity of the cheapest meat that it could and the regular stews served up were evidence of this.

When you then add to the equation the rather inconvenient half-basement kitchens and the small Dining Hall which meant back-to-back sittings for lunch if some of the day boys were to be fed as well as the boarders, the problems faced daily by the domestic staff begin to come into focus. There was a core of full-time people, but also a largely unrecognised (by the boys) army of ladies who came in for the lunch period to help prepare vegetables and do the washing-up. A lot depended on them and Jean Scragg recalled the panic in the ranks if the message arrived with her that a couple of the regulars were off sick or had priority engagements and she and anyone else who could be press-ganged had to swing into action at short notice!

Apart from this was the need to account for every cup of tea or other snack so as to be able to reclaim costs and coupons. This gives a taste of the feeding of the masses from the providers' end of things. Were the difficulties and effort put into overcoming them appreciated by the consumers?

There was quite a crowd in the bar of the Star. Apart from the lunchtime regulars, some twenty Old Boys from the 1940s had arranged to meet up and had kindly invited me to join them. Food clearly still mattered and whatever else advancing years had eroded, appetite seemed not to be amongst them.

"Now that is what I call a sausage!" said one, eying his neighbour's plate, "It would have made breakfast for half the table in the good old days."

"I know this will sound odd, but I really rather liked the school sausages. True, they were probably 90% bread and were pretty small, but they were among my favourites. You needed to get one which was browned all over though."

"What I could never understand was why most mornings at breakfast you could smell bacon and eggs, but never actually saw, let alone ate, any. We always said that the staff either ate our rations or sold them off on the black market, but there was that smell and although the staff table had special thin toast, I never saw them with bacon and eggs."

"No hope of toast for us! Just slogs. I must say that we didn't go short there, although you had to work pretty hard to stuff yourself in the twenty minutes you had. The problem there was that you ran out of things to put on them. After the war the marge seemed to run out half way through the week and we got slogs without. We called them 'nudes'."

"Someone used to keep a tally on the wall of how many days each week we had nudes. Wally Bale, wasn't it?"

"Now there was a nutter if you like! Do you remember that squirrel he found and kept in his dormitory locker? He tried to play with the thing under the bed clothes and there was this great yell as it bit him. Blood everywhere! Can't remember what happened to the squirrel, but he had to pretend to Matron that he had had a nose-bleed to explain the blood on his sheets."

"His mate, 'Smokey' Joe Buckland, was just as crazy. There was that lovely incident with Johnny Scragg when he wanted to make some announcement in the playground and sent a junior to fetch the old hand-bell he used when getting attention and quiet. Trouble was that he always called the bell 'Cracked Joe' because it had a crack in the metal. The junior didn't know that when asked to fetch Cracked Joe, but raced away and came back with Buckland!"

"You could always put a bit of jam on a nude."

"I beg your pardon!! Oh, you've gone back to slogs! Well, yes you could – if you had any left. It was just one jar each a month. If you held your knife vertical, dipped it straight in and pulled it straight out, you could almost make it last the month and still get a faint taste on the slog. It was pretty amazing too how much jam a hungry junior could get out of a completely empty jam jar!"

"I only remember two kinds of jam. There was gooseberry jam, or 'frogspawn' and then plum which we called 'red axle grease' – or 'red stone, plum-less'. They were OK. Once, Rosenthal and some others went picking blackberries on the Downs and brought a lot back. I don't know where the sugar came from, but the kitchen made jam out of them and that was good."

"Blackberries were pretty civilised things for a boarder to bring in! Wasn't it Cox who went fishing in the town drain or something and brought back what looked like four diseased sticklebacks and insisted that they be cooked for his tea? They did it too and he lived. A boarder's stomach must be lined with stainless steel!"

"We used to spread school mustard on slogs when we ran out of everything else. I am amazed that no-one was sick!"

"I certainly remember those bowls of mustard pickle which we had and putting the pickles on slogs. We were always hungry and I used to eat my toothpaste, but then my Mum made sure I changed to Colgate dentifrice which came in an inedible solid block!"

"Some of the boys versed in countryside traditions used to put some milk into bottles with stoppers to them and shake the milk to make butter which we spread on the bread. The trouble was that it took an age for the butter to be formed and you probably used up more energy making it than you gained by eating it!"

"That's interesting," I said, "We did that too up until about 1953. After that the craze just died out. I never really trusted myself to eat it though. Anyway, it was hard to get the stuff out of the bottle and we didn't have to economise in quite the same way that you did."

"Some of us didn't bother to economise either! I never saw McCarthy's jam last much longer than a week. He had enough pocket money to buy things like peanut butter and extras like pork pies and as his home was only just over the hill in Lancing, he could always stock up there if his mother let him."

"Although I was a day boy, as a senior prefect I would sometimes stay overnight to help with the fire watching and so would go to breakfast with the boarders. There always seemed to be kippers when I was there and, of course, slogs. I rather liked it all, perhaps because of the novelty as much as for the food. The day boys met slogs at first break too when we had slogs and a third of a pint of milk. However, it was good to be able to use my privileged position to go out into the town at lunch time and get a really nice lunch of Welsh rarebit on toast for ninepence!"

"That was cheap! Baked beans on toast was one and nine in the restaurant by the Clock Tower in the High Street. I used to buy it when I was in funds."

"I used to go to the café by the Old Market Hall on Wednesday lunch hour for tea and a cake which cost 3d."

"Most of us didn't have much cash. I remember Hammond working out what he would get with his sixpence pocket money and, if I have got it right it came to a loaf of bread for tuppence-ha'penny, a quarter of marge for another tuppence-ha'penny and ten orange balls for a penny. He didn't have a tuck box either, being a refugee, which made it even harder to get by. Most of us would have gone without the marge and have got two loaves. We used to sit on the wall by the bakery, or go up Mouse Lane and pig ourselves just pulling the bread apart with our hands. I can still taste it when I think about it."

"And there speaks a man with a mouthful of roast chicken! Do you remember ever eating chicken at school? I can't even remember eating it at home unless it was at Christmas. Now there is a change between then and now!"

"No, we didn't get chicken, but we did get rabbit stew! Rabbits weren't rationed. Scraggy liked going shooting and I think he was allowed to shoot rabbits anywhere on the Wiston Estate. Anyway with him blasting away all over the Downs and probably the school buying rabbits from anyone who had shot or snared them, we were no strangers to rabbit stew. It was pretty good, but I haven't had any since I left. We seem to have swapped over these days, from rabbit to chicken!"

"I seem to remember that you could buy a rabbit from the butcher for a bob. The school may have had them cheaper."

"I haven't had rabbit stew since then either. It was loathsome stuff and I hated it."

"You were a day bug and could afford to be choosey! Anyway, I thought that you said that you were in the Rabbit Club and wasn't that supposed to be part of the war effort for food?"

"It may have been the idea, but we just treated them like pets. We never ate any of ours. We did sell them in the market though, so I expect a lot were eaten in the end."

"It was a good skive getting rabbit food. We quite often went as far as Shoreham by the Coombes road supposedly collecting greenery. We would then try to cadge some tea from Scoones's mother, after having done some plane-spotting at Shoreham airport. I used to go to the kitchens for any old cabbage leaves too and used to scoff the off-cut crusts from the staff's toast. As good as biscuits that was! We had a bit of fun too. There was one time when we were waiting for our lot of rabbits to be auctioned in the market and it was getting close to lunch, so one of us, and I can't recall who, could have been Brown, tried to hurry things along by bidding for a calf which was the lot before ours. The farmers said to the auctioneer, 'Go on. Let the lad have it!' and so he got the calf for a couple of bob. We smuggled it back behind the gym, fed it and sold it in the next week's market for a huge profit!"

"Our back garden at home looked like Old MacDonald's farmyard! We took self-sufficiency seriously – chickens, rabbits, ducks, turkeys and even a goat. Once when the weather was really bad, a group of us took shelter in the market to wait for our train home to arrive. Very few people had turned up and a good number of lots had found no buyer. I got a dozen day-old chicks for a tanner and got them home without the poor mites freezing to death, much to my mother's surprise!"

"Sounds a bit like our garden. We kept chickens basically for the eggs, but heaven help any poor layers! I can remember the excitement when a neighbour had a pig slaughtered – under strict controls, I have no doubt – and the meat was shared out. I expect we either paid for it or bartered it, but all I was interested in was eating it! My mother used beetroot when she couldn't find lipstick. People got pretty ingenious."

"People did get prosecuted, you know, if they were caught slaughtering an animal for their own use. There was a rhyme about some farmer in Scotland, I think, who killed and ate a sheep: *There's no wether on the tether/ Where the wether used to be,/ But there's chops upon the rafters/ That Lord Woolton mustn't see./ They say it was the weather/ That the wether couldn't stand./ It died of influenza,/ But the smell of it was grand.* The play on words amused me at the time which is why I remember it."

"Who was Lord Woolton? The owner of the estate?"

"No,no! He was the Minister for Food!"

"Well, I give the school kitchen full marks considering rationing and all that. I liked most of the food – I do make an exception of the macaroni cheese which I simply could not eat, but I did make sure that I sat next to someone who did like it and swap for something like kippers which he didn't like when they came on to the menu. The puddings were especially good."

"The stodges were good, I agree, but what about that stuff we called 'slobber' which they made with ground rice and milk! It was pretty disgusting. Then once I think there was something which was supposed to have set solid, but which didn't so they warmed it all up and stirred in some cocoa powder. That was awful too! I wasn't keen on the sago pudding or that frog spawn muck – tapioca, was it? Still, people did eat it and survived."

"Whatever you say, we were pretty healthy and fit. Those at the school in Bolton's reign said that the food then was like Dotheboys Hall's and that things only really improved when we had to get to grips with rationing. I gather that there were all sorts of information sheets and things like that which gave good ideas, even if it was all pretty basic. Sometimes someone used their imagination too. I remember the revolt when we had rice pudding when the sugar had run out and there was no sweetness to it at all. Mr Bowman went rampaging into the kitchens and came out with a great bag of sultanas which he dished out into the plates to loud cheers!"

"It wasn't just things like jam and sugar which were short. About half way through the war, Matron organised a sort of shop for used clothes and I got a second-hand blazer from it. It didn't fit too well and was a bit worn, but I was glad to have it. There was no way I would have got a blazer otherwise."

"The clothes which I outgrew got passed on in the family or to friends and most of what I did wear had been handed down from older boys in the same way. No wonder that the rules about school uniform were relaxed! We must have looked an odd bunch of scruffs!"

"I always hated having to select from cast-off clothes, but was happy enough to appear in public wearing the 'new' blazer, or whatever."

"It was all 'make-do and mend' too. It was very hard to find material, my mother told me. Everyone had holes in their jackets and trousers and I used to be glad to get them home for my mother to mend. Matron tended to go pop if she thought that you had been careless!"

"You couldn't get cups or mugs easily either, and we used the jam jars for the school tea – 'dishwater'! The art was to find the tea hot enough to crack the jam jar. Floods of tea of course. The maids must have loved us!"

"Some of the maids were very nice too!"

"Come along! You must have been all of ten years old then!"

"Carnal appetites develop early in war time, old chap! Anyway, it was all very innocent or wishful thinking, even amongst the seniors."

"There were quite a lot of girls around, even though we were under orders not to talk to them. Of course, everyone did, but with the Canadian soldiers about the place, it was only the younger girls we could nab. The older ones knew on which side their bread was buttered! Yes, and naming no names, there were a few 'town bicycles'!"

"It wasn't only the soldiers who could jump the queue! I remember SBS giving us all a lecture on the village girls; how they were forbidden fruit so far as we were concerned; and how we would be whacked if we were found in close proximity to any. Then shortly after, we bumped into him in the High Street with a pretty girl on his arm. We touched our caps to him and I had to say 'I bet you don't get the whack, sir!' to which he replied, 'No, but you will!' Of course, nothing happened."

"I suppose that given the company assembled, the conversation had soon to descend from the misty realms of higher thought to basics!"

"Anyone who thinks that chat about slogs and second-hand blazers comprises higher thought fully deserves the Astonishing Revelations which are clearly about to be made by Those Who Knew Him in His Youth. With any luck, your wife will have finished her shopping in time to join us! Question is where shall we start?"

"McCarthy's detective agency, perhaps?"

"That was Rosenthal's fault really, because he paid McCarthy a cigarette to spy on a group of girls to try to get incriminating evidence to be used to Rosenthal's advantage."

"The Sylvia Carrington gang?"

"Got it in one! Anyway, it soon got messy with McCarthy practising his spying and shadowing techniques on Sylvia, Betty Mighell and Sheila Tuck. They caught on more or less at once and gave him a bit of a run. He said he was puzzled why Betty gave him a dirty look! Then he more or less fell over Jackers Routh with Eileen Goddard and got roundly cursed by them. Next day he managed to trail the wrong lot of girls and by this time had stirred things up nicely! He had a row with his 'employer' after a girl he wanted to see didn't turn up on the train and they both got teased by Sylvia, Sheila and Irene Ide who kept tapping on their window. Then, amazingly, Sheila Tuck asked him to go for a walk with her. He, of course, was too clever for his own good and, trying not to seem too eager, said he would perhaps another time. Then when he asked her the next day, she gave him the raspberry by saying it was too late. He always reckoned it was a lucky brush-off because, just when she was beginning to change her mind, Freda Sage swept round the corner together with the whole of the Junior Walk. He said that he was across the road in two hops, wishing to keep his reputation for saintliness! Some saint!"

"How long did all this go on for?"

"All the time, so far as I can remember. It all just rumbled on week after week with more and more girls getting stirred up and more and more boys having their private lives exposed to view. No-one actually killed him and I can't think why. Just when you were getting somewhere (you hoped!), up bobbed McCarthy from behind a bush or a barn. The funny thing was that everyone wanted his information and so he did a brisk trade."

"I suppose that he did well in other ways too!"

"Well, he certainly enjoyed talking to the girls, but at our age then, the best you could really hope for was a kiss or hold hands. It was amazingly innocent. He told me that he wished that Sheila, the light of his life at the time, would wear her green slacks again – because they made him nearly die laughing! Not much romance there!"

"He told me once that there were only about three girls left in Steyning who would talk to him, but he would have to step up his tart-chasing if he was to stay Steyning's Public Enemy No. 1. He reckoned that while he was no good as a steady boyfriend, he was hot stuff as a girl chaser. Anyway, he knew that Jackers Routh had eight different girlfriends one after the other – had the cheek to say that Jackers ought to settle down! Then, off he'd go for an afternoon's snooping!"

"Well, he put all this trailing and spying to good use later on."

"How come?"

"Didn't you know that he wrote dozens of books and his Johnny Fedora ones were published ahead of the much later James Bond books by Fleming? He was a Professor of English, but he wrote novels under the pen name of Desmond Cory. Google him up and you'll be surprised at all he wrote. I think that I am right in saying that he even had one book published while he was still at school. He certainly wrote several 'books' while he was at Steyning and was pretty sensitive about people trying to read them. I remember him telling me that he was out to show G.K. Chesterton and Agatha Christie who was who!"

"There was the 'No Girls' rule, but no-one took much notice. You just kept an eye out for the staff. The librarians and prefects were a bit of a danger to boarders trying to slip out in the evenings, but they often had girls in mind too!"

"Even the day boys had to watch it a bit if they lived in Steyning! The staff took a dim view if they saw you talking to girls. The boys coming from Henfield, Shoreham, Storrington and so on, had no problems – other than trying to get the girl you were interested in to get interested in you! As someone said just now, it was OK if you were in the middle school and after girls of say fourteen to sixteen, but if you were in the 6th Form and were after the older ones, you stood no chance most of the time with the soldiers around. Still, we managed somehow – even the boarders! All this talk about boys schools being a nest of 'unnatural vices' is a lot of tosh if you try to apply it to SGS in the 40s. All that being a boarder meant was that going out with girls took a bit of ingenuity, some common sense and the spirit of adventure. You got pretty expert in giving plausible excuses too!"

"Jackers Routh used to give evening prayers a miss sometimes to go out. The one time anyone raised questions, he said that he had been in the Bog. The cream of the jest was that he had been in the Bog that time and Matron could confirm that he had an upset tum! Some people are just born lucky."

"You had to take chances sometimes. The competition for the prettiest girls was pretty fierce, even without taking the soldiers into account. Take Jean Gray for example….."

"Wish I could have! She was a cracker!"

"Down, Fido!"

"…..everyone was chasing her and just when you thought she had settled on one boy, she would be with another. They used to steal her from one another and you had to be on your toes. One minute she was with Kitchener, the next with Routh and so on. To tell the truth, she was the one calling the shots whatever any of us thought."

" She wasn't the one who gave someone the brush-off by saying that she was now going out with a doctor and had no time any more for schoolboys in caps, was she?"

"I didn't hear that one. A bit cruel if true!"

"What about the other end of the scale then? That could be amusing - and cruel in its way too."

"What do you mean?"

"Form 1! They used to chase the little girls in the primary school and would talk to them over the fence and wall between our playgrounds. They got cursed by the staff of both schools and by our prefects, for doing so. Some of them would throw notes over and little Dicky Wiseman got caught out! Someone in the Cleaning-up Squad found a note which Dicky's beloved had sent across and it ended up with John Scragg. He took it into Assembly; gave a speech about the evils of wasting paper; and then read it out. Poor Dicky! It pledged her undying affection and assured him that 'my chest is much better now', which could be taken in about a hundred different ways - and was - by the rest of us. How embarrassing! If it had been me, I would have felt like kicking JS in a painful place. Still, it was very funny from our point of view."

"It is things like that which can put boys off girls for life."

"Maybe so, but I didn't notice anything like that with Dicky. He just learnt to be more careful – or got his lady friend to be so!"

"Talking of lady friends, it looks as though the shopping expedition is returning to base. It appears that you will not now have the money to buy me a drink, old boy, so let me do the honours! Mrs C, can I offer you a bit of refreshment? Funnily enough, we were talking about 'girl friends past' as you came in. John can tell you all about it while I get the drinks."

CHAPTER 4

Getting ready

In the early part of the war there was a flurry of activity at local level preparing for air raids and possible invasion. Although everyone took it very seriously, an element of farce was never far away and the popular TV comedy series of recent years, *Dad's Army,* holds more than a grain of truth. Even in *Dad's Army* no-one had to ask, as really happened, a neighbouring Home Guard unit to lend them the one rifle available in the area so that their members could see how it worked before there was any invasion. Lewis Wood, an Old Boy and member of the Home Guard in Steyning, records that when an invasion was thought likely, they had a post on the top of the Round Hill and the Commander said: "If there is an invasion, I shall need someone to run from the Round Hill to Steyning to warn them." Lewis replied: "Sir, if there is anybody doing any running, I'll do it!" He also tells that when the church bells were rung in 1940 after a false alarm, he was issued with a rifle and five rounds of ammunition and told to guard the telephone exchange. However, there was plenty of initiative around even though arms were scarce. The Henfield Home Guard invaded Steyning successfully in a field exercise. In the return match, Steyning infiltrated the Henfield defences in a hearse. When Henfield cried foul play, Steyning pointed out that Hitler used unfair tactics too; the umpires agreed and allowed the victory.

It is a matter for regret that a full-scale practice attack on Steyning involving aircraft dropping flour-bombs, troops and tanks testing the town's defences (of about one tank trap and a pill-box!) and lots of volunteer 'casualties' never took place, although it was planned for and advertised. The school would have joined in with a good deal of enthusiasm! Whether the boys would have made more patient 'casualties' than one man did in a practice in another area is doubtful. After a long delay waiting for 'medical attention' he wrote a note which he tied to the post he had been propped against, reading 'Have bled to death and gone home'. Another practice which did take place in Steyning was laid on by the fire brigade which, in front of an attentive audience, set some magnesium alight to show what an incendiary bomb would be like. A fireman then played a hose on it while the Fire Chief explained that although the man should have been lying down, this would have to be imagined because each fireman had but one uniform issued and he wanted to keep it looking nice!

One of the first things to happen was preparation of air raid trenches and proper shelters and the organisation of air raid wardens and fire-watchers locally. ARP practices were carried out at the school at various times, including one at 11.00pm for the boarders in which the dormitories were evacuated in 4 minutes. Gas was thought to be a real threat and, in addition to the issue of gas masks, which had to be carried at all times out of Steyning, although stored in lockers when inside the town, gas-proof shelters were organised, especially for places such as boarding schools. In Steyning, the Lower Corridor was closed off by partitions at either end to give a safe area and, in the first few months of the war all the boarders slept there on thin mattresses and in some kind of a sleeping bag which parents were asked to provide. In the day time, the mattresses were stacked in the corridor near to the stairs coming down from Big School. Later on, when gas was no longer seen as a major threat and it was evident that Steyning was not to be a focus of attack by bombers, the boarders took to the designated safe parts of the buildings at night only when there was an air raid warning and gas masks were virtually abandoned. Slit trenches were dug on the edge of the playing field by the police station where the school played its games so that people could find shelter immediately if there was a hit-and-run raid. These were soon filled in because the threat from the air never materialised and they accumulated litter.

On the south side of the field was an Observer Corps post. At first they used microphones mounted in parabolic dishes to pick up the sound of approaching aircraft, but these were scrapped once the radar station at Poling became fully operational. In the steep-sided coombe in the Downs from which the springs feeding the mill-pond flowed, the old rifle range was refurbished. The entrance was along a track near the junction of Mouse Lane with the High Street and the boys were not supposed to enter it. Need I say that the rifle range was a popular venue! The dip slope of the Downs above Steyning, as they ran towards the sea, sprouted a profusion of odd-looking structures, the purpose of which was to deter planes or gliders from landing in the event of an invasion. This whole area was soon requisitioned as a battle training area which was heavily used from about 1941 through to the D-Day landings.

Over the course of the first years of the war, searchlights and anti-aircraft batteries were installed, but mainly to the south where bombing raids were not infrequent, especially so in Shoreham and Littlehampton where there were harbours. Pill boxes were put up at strategic points along the roads and the railway, the one at Bramber Station masquerading as a café! Tank traps were constructed with fiendish enthusiasm and specially constructed systems of pipes leading from oil tanks buried near the roadside were installed so that flaming barriers could be ignited to protect the downland fortress proposed between the Round Hill and Chanctonbury Ring. One of these was on the Bostal Road at its steepest and the oil tanks were concealed in the small chalk pit where the recent excavation to put them in was not noticeable in a place with a lot of bare chalk already in it. It was here that one of the West brothers lit a match to see what was inside the tanks. His burns were only minor, but he lost his eyebrows, eye lashes and a lot of hair and had to wear a skull-cap for a while to cover his baldness. Nearer the town along the Bostal Road and in a larger chalk pit which housed disused lime kilns, two 9.2-inch howitzers were installed. These First World War veterans were brought in pieces from East Sussex, reconstructed and laid so as to cover the entry approaches to Shoreham harbour. They had a range of about nine miles and were very accurate with their 300lb shells. The Navy got quite annoyed, in fact, when their target raft was smashed to smithereens in practice firing. When practice took place, anyone living nearby was warned to open their windows in the hope that they would not then be broken by the report of the guns. Smaller howitzers were placed at intervals along the south-facing slopes of the Downs, ranged just off the beaches. Since the existing bridges over the railway at Bramber and over the river at Beeding were thought too weak to carry tanks, the Sappers constructed Bailey bridges later in the war to take such traffic on its way to Shoreham harbour. Early in the war the iron bridge over the river off Kings Barn Lane was repainted black to make it less conspicuous from the air. Previously know as the White Bridge, it now became known as the Iron Bridge and has remained black ever since.

In the town itself, communal air raid shelters were soon put up and each served a particular part of the town. One shelter survives in Wykeham Close – Communal Shelter No. 5 - , and is now being used as a garage. Steyning was divided into six sectors and each of these was subdivided into two or three areas, each covered by a warden.

The wardens most closely affecting the school were Fred Laker, publican of the Norfolk Arms, who looked after the north side of Church Street and W.G. Theobald from Wykeham Close, who was in charge of the north side of School Lane. Another ARP Warden was Mr Thomson, the chemist. He had a side-line in making Molotov cocktails for the Home Guard and the chalk pit off Newham Lane at the foot of the Round Hill was used as a practice range for them. In anticipation of its need, warranted perhaps by this activity as well as the threat of enemy action, a new fire-engine was acquired by the town's fire brigade. Unfortunately, no-one had thought to note its dimensions. When it arrived, it was found that it would not fit into the fire station under the clock tower, even when the ladder was removed, and it had to be kept in the yard of the Chequer Inn.

The school seemed to look after itself, with its own arrangements for shelter, and with the senior boys, including the day boy school prefects, and the staff sharing fire-watching duties at night. There were three air raid shelters built in the school grounds, one next to Dormer and alongside School Lane and two in the playground – one close to the woodwork shop, between it and the gym; the other near to the wall separating the grammar school from the primary school and between the playground trees and the gym. The war was about two years old before these shelters were put up. In some parts of Britain the local authorities had rebelled against the idea that lower standards of construction be applied to school air raid shelters than to those for the public at large and this delayed their provision altogether! In the meantime, blackout curtains had to be made and fitted. Light-shades which resembled cocoa tins were fitted to the lights giving a downwards and subdued light. All the windows were painted with a transparent rubber solution to prevent their splintering in any blast.

It was even later in the war that the school formed a Cadet Corps, but the Scouts were involved in the Home Guard as messengers, not only in Steyning, but also in all the areas from which day boys came. For this service they were paid pocket money, something never despised by schoolboys! When the Cadets were up and running, the most senior were also appointed as Home Guards. Some of the staff were in the Home Guard too and one boy found himself in the glorious position of being in charge of a section which had a member of staff in it!

One member of staff was involved with a far darker force than the Home Guard and John Scragg's activities are outlined in Chapter 5.

Geoffrey Mason, Head Boy from1942/43 and 1943/44, Rodney Cox, a fellow boarder with Geoffrey from 1939-1945 and I had arranged to have coffee with Jean Scragg and then go on to have a bite of lunch before returning home. Once everyone had got settled and news exchanged about recently encountered Old Boys, Jean recalled an early meeting with Geoffrey.

"I was being shown round the school late one evening and when we got to the path running by the Headmaster's study I noticed a boy in a sleeping bag on that little tiled 'veranda' by the French windows. The head peeping out said, very politely, 'Good evening!' and I discovered that it was Geoffrey on fire-watching duty. It was explained that the prefects, librarians and the staff shared this chore and although the flat roof over the classrooms was used as a look-out post, the Headmaster's study, where there was a telephone, was the focal point of the operation."

"That's quite right. We worked it in shifts. There were two bunk beds in the classroom next to the HM's study, Room 8, one for the duty master and the other for the duty prefect on fire-watching. When it was warm and fine, I'd sleep out on the lawn or, as Jean saw, outside the study. We also had to take charge if an air-raid warning was given and make sure that the boarders were in the safe parts of the buildings. That was why the fire-watchers slept near to the telephone in the Headmaster's study which was used to give the warning signals of 'green', 'amber', or 'red'. If it was 'red', then the boarders had to be shifted from the dormitories to the safe parts of the buildings. The proper shelters didn't go up until about 1942 and I only recall them being used once in my days, when the bomb fell in Church Street. The safe areas were Lower Corridor; the corridor on the ground floor of Dormer; or the half-basement in Coombe Court. Lower Corridor could be quite a hazard, especially if you wanted to find the lavatory. You couldn't use any light and it was pitch black. The perfect setting for painful chaos if you were a junior treading on seniors' faces on the way to the Bog! When we were all afraid early in the war that gas might be used, **everyone** had to go to Lower Corridor, which was the gas shelter, and that was most uncomfortable."

"There is a remark in the School Magazine for 1944/45," I said, "That nights in the summer were disrupted by doodlebugs and that masters and boys had to sleep in the shelters. It says that they all hated the shelters, but got some satisfaction from seeing the staff having to rough it too!"

"I remember someone saying that when he was in Long Dorm, he was taken into the kitchens for shelter and loved it because it was a lot warmer than the dormitory! I never went there myself though."

"I'm pretty sure that no-one used the kitchen in my time, but I only got deeply involved in the lives of the boarders when John became Head in 1944. By that time the air-raid shelters were up and being used."

"Do you know, I remember seeing the workmen start building the shelters in the playground. They simply spread a sheet of builders' tarpaulin on the tarmac surface and built on top of it, so far as I could see. It always puzzled me because I thought that they should have good foundations. I had this splendid mental picture of the shelters being blown along the playground with all the boarders inside if a bomb were to go off nearby."

"That would have been quite a sight!"

"You mentioned that we couldn't use lights. Did I ever tell you about Mr Savage, the caretaker, getting the school fined? No? Well, he was terrifically hard-working and late one evening was cleaning and checking over boarders' shoes in his little cubby-hole off Lower Corridor, using just one light pulled well down and with a dim bulb under the cocoa-tin shade. There was no way anyone could have seen the light from above, but the warden, looking down the service passage to the kitchens from Church Street saw it. The school was fined £10 and Savage was furious! The warden was Fred Laker too, from the Norfolk Arms whom we knew well!"

"Of course Mr Savage was one of two caretakers when I was at school in the 1950s. Mr Nash was the other."

"Nash was there well before the war, I believe – Geoffrey would remember – but was called up and Savage, who was unfit for military service, replaced him. He had at one time worked in the London Docks and kept one habit we couldn't cure. He would spit on the ground when talking to you, especially if he was complaining about something. When John was Head, he would come storming into his study sometimes, usually complaining about 'them perfects' as he always called the prefects and every time he said 'them perfects' he would spit. John would come round to Holland Cottage and say 'I'm afraid that Savage has been to see me again, dear!' and I would collect a bucket, disinfectant and a floor-cloth and go over to mop up!"

"I can confirm that Mr Nash was a caretaker when I came in 1936 and there was another, Mr Gardener. Gardener left in 1937 and was replaced by Mr Mullins, who I think came from Weymouth College with Mr Stuart-Clark."

"Mullins must have been well before my time as well as Gardener. I don't recall them at all. Mr Nash I got to know only after the war. He was a very pleasant man. Savage, of course, made much of the fact that while he, the unfit man, had spent six years of single-handed hard labour keeping the school going, Nash, the fit man, had spent six years on a seaside holiday in Dorset with a searchlight battery and free meals thrown in. They seemed to get on well though."

"It strikes me that a Headmaster's wife in those days did a bit more than would be expected now!"

"That may well be so. However, when John became Head, I was expected to do something to help. We were determined not to go back to the Bolton days where Mrs was openly involved with managing the boys. John wanted my role to be under the boys' radar and so I was in charge of all the domestic staff and that side of things. That was not all, and into the 1950s John and I would roll our sleeves up in the holidays and try to get plaster and paintwork renovated so that the place looked reasonable for the start of term. There was little labour available and, anyway, the school could not afford it."

"That explains the draconian sanctions applied by your husband in the early 1950s and which I well recall, should anyone be found damaging the paintwork in places like Wykeham!"

"Did you ever know, Jean, that when John became Headmaster, there was a rumour that he had married you because a Headmaster had to be married?"

"That is so funny! Do you know that after we married in 1943, we spent a lot of time discussing whether he should go on with teaching? He was thinking of going back to doing anthropological research. When the offer was made, it helped that we were married because, as we were hinting, the Governors got two members of staff for the price of one! However, nothing was further from our thoughts in 1943 when we all assumed that the Stuart-Clarks would be with us for a long time. It was quite a shock when he told us he was going as Head to Brighton College at very short notice. He actually took some of the admin. staff with him, including our Matron, Miss Armitage, or rather Mrs Gardner as she had become, so there was a bit of emergency recruitment for me to do straight away. Then Stanley Bayliss Smith followed him next year as Head of the Junior School at Brighton College and it was John's turn to find a replacement. Tom Pretheroe was his first appointment and never one he regretted."

"I went to Brighton College to teach under SBS after my first stint in the Army. I was there long enough to think that teaching was not really for me and rejoined the Army as a career soldier. I found out from John, you know, that when Stuart-Clark made me Head Boy in 1942/43, he advised against it and was disappointed when his advice was not followed. He was big enough not only to tell me that, but also to say that his judgement had been badly astray. That was during my second year as Head Boy in 1943/44. It was something I always tried to remember when I found my own judgement similarly off-beam."

"Jean, do you know much about the first few years of the war at the school?"

"Well, obviously I heard quite a lot from John, although we had other things to talk about, as you may imagine, which were more interesting to both of us! But it was only after we were married that I had any first-hand experience and that was not until 1943. The initial flapping around was a long way behind us then and the school seemed to run as if little was happening outside. We even did rather well under rationing to get palatable and nourishing food on the table for the boarders and any day boys taking school lunch. There were a one or two calamities, but on the whole it was a smooth operation and we had few complaints from the boys or parents. The parents knew how difficult it could be and the boys were hungry enough to eat almost anything – even though they all suspected that the staff ate their rations, which they did not, of course! No, I think that I will have to disappoint you, George, over the earlier part of the war. Geoffrey and Rodney are far more reliable sources!"

"How about the later developments such as the Cadet Corps?"

"Ah, yes! It was 'Stinky' Bowman who was in charge of that. In fact, I believe that he originated the idea. You can't imagine anyone less military than he was to look at, short, a bit stout and very untidy, but I understand that he put heart and soul into the Corps and had them well organised. The Corps was popular with the senior boys because of the shooting and 'dangerous' games. Some were in the Home Guard too because they were NCOs in the Cadets and there was high status to be gained, turning up at school in uniform and, in the later days, armed with a rifle!"

"I recall that when the Bow was living in No. 7, he built a pond in the garden with the help of the boys and lined it with concrete. There was a fountain connected by lab. tubing to a reservoir in the staff room, which was directly above it on the first floor. I can't remember whether there was a pump to recycle the water. He may just have filled the reservoir from a tap when it ran dry. I wonder how long that pond lasted."

"Well it was certainly there all through the 1950s! The concrete had cracked but we used to repair it and clean everything out from time to time and restock it from ponds around Steyning. The biology masters would then use it as a source of specimens for classes, so it earned its keep. There was no fountain in my days and the staff room was by then the School Prefects' Room."

"Good heavens! When did the prefects take over?"

"About 1953 I think."

"More change and decay, eh?"

"I would have you know, Rodney, that not only did our domestic staff work hard at keeping the decay to a minimum, but also that John and I rolled our sleeves up in the holidays, as I told you. The No. 7 pond was not one of the priority jobs! Anyway, John needed a few dirty jobs in store and pond cleaning was a welcome addition to gardening, weeding the Headmaster's Lawn and litter picking!"

"Ah, litter picking was definitely an early war-time task. The Cleaning-up Squads were there to save paper going to waste as well as making the place look tidy. It was usually the smallest boys, Forms 1 and 2, who were the core of the Squads because it involved little physical strength. It was not just the playground and corridors which were covered, but also the Playing Field and sometimes there was a general foray into the town. Usually though, the Squads operated over smaller areas where the prefects could keep an eye on them. I remember when we were strung out in a line across the Playing Field the message came down the line 'Headmaster has lost a tanner. Pass it on.'"

"We still had general litter picks in the 50s when the whole school would be told in Assembly that the place was disgustingly dirty and that since it was we who had made it so, the whole of the morning break would be spent picking up litter. This was usually followed by the rider that the bit behind the gym was particularly bad and that under no circumstances whatsoever was litter to be thrown over the fence into the private gardens."

"That was often because John had received complaints from the owners of those gardens. They were particularly sensitive to boys climbing over without permission to retrieve balls."

"Well that goes back into the 1930s! There were one or two boys with exceptionally strong kicks in playground football who could boot a tennis ball right over the gym and into those gardens. Don Chalk was one and Ron Ayling another. More often the ball stayed on the gym roof and every so often a ladder would be got from the caretakers and someone went up to restore the collection of balls to ground level. We didn't often have the same problem with playground cricket which was played with the wicket painted on the iron railings at the top of the playground."

"That's interesting and shows how traditions get handed on. A photo taken in about 1905 shows a wicket painted on the brickwork of a broad arch leading into the playground from the Big School stairs. This was destroyed during the building works which were completed in 1912, giving the Lower and Upper Corridors in their first form; set up the school bathrooms next to Big School, which by the late 1930s had lockers for the day boys replace the baths, leaving only the washbasins behind; and added the classrooms which in the 1940s were a laboratory and Rooms 4 and 5. The wicket was then moved sideways a bit on to the iron railings."

"The main hazard in playground cricket was the Headmaster's Lawn – six and out and a mission to find John for permission to get the ball back. Permission always granted, but unauthorised forays were frowned on and lawn weeding the likely outcome! The other usual problem was getting the ball wedged high up between a down-pipe from the gutter and the wall on the classroom block. The person who shinned up to get it back was allowed to bat next."

"The other peculiarity in playground cricket was 'snags'. You could pair up with someone and you operated as a single person, so if one of you won the right to bat by getting someone out, you both batted one after the other. The ardent desire of any keen junior was to persuade someone in the school's First X1 to agree to be your snag! A rare, but sought after favour!"

There was a brief pause before Jean said firmly, "Well, it has been lovely to see you all and have had this chat. I have enjoyed it. Now, before you go you must have a look at the garden. George, you are the tallest, so would you pick up the secateurs as we go through the kitchen and you can dead-head some roses which I can't reach."

CHAPTER 5

Scallywagging

Jean had made reference to John's war-time activities and as we walked down to the Chequer, Rodney said that we ought to have asked her more because he was a bit in the dark about just what John had been doing as a member of an Auxiliary Unit.

"I doubt that you would have learnt a great deal from her," I said, "It was all pretty secret, except for one brief period, and auxiliaries were supposed to conceal what they were up to, even from their families. They were in a very high risk job as it was and the fewer who knew any details, the less information could be given away under interrogation. The bits which she did know about – or at least the bits she was prepared to disclose - are in Stewart Angell's book. That is all that she has ever told me too. But I have been doing some reading about these special units and could run over the main points when we have lunch if you like. It does explain quite a bit about Johnny's character and behaviour I'll think you'll agree."

The pub was surprisingly quiet and we got a table in a corner and ordered lunch and drinks. Once settled, Geoffrey said, "I would be interested to hear about what you have learnt about the Auxiliaries. Even to a professional soldier, albeit of a later vintage, it was all very mysterious. I have a vague feeling that the Special Operations Executive was involved. At the time, we had no idea of what John was up to, other that he was in the Home Guard and would sometimes appear in class in uniform. The authorities kept the wraps on for 50 years and it was only in the 90s that things began to appear in print."

"From what I can gather, they are still very reticent and although by now a bit threadbare, the Cloak of Secrecy is still wound round some aspects of the case and there is a good deal of kicking and screaming if anyone tries to pull off these sad rags. That is to say that, in the best Civil Service tradition, some of the relevant documents have unfortunately, been lost/inadvertently destroyed/ burned in the blitz/would disclose information prejudicial to the safety of the realm and so on."

"It seems odd that anything which a bunch of Home Guards got up to sixty years back should warrant this scale of official secrecy."

"Now, you have run off the rails at the first bend! Col. Frank Douglas reported after the war that: 'To compare the Auxiliary Units with the Home Guard is like comparing the Brigade of Guards with the Salvation Army.' They were a very different bunch of people. Put at its most brutal, they were small, clandestine groups of trained assassins whose job was, should a successful invasion be achieved, to let it sweep over them and to emerge later to act as mosquito troops operating not only against Germans by setting booby-traps and committing acts of sabotage, but also and importantly, liquidating any countrymen suspected of collaboration or known to possess information which would be helpful to an enemy if disclosed under interrogation or torture. One Unit had identified their own Group Commander (itself a post generated by a well-meaning but misguided policy put into practice in the middle of the Auxiliary Units' period of operation) as their number one target because he knew the location of all the Operational Bases and identity of all the Unit leaders and could compromise their existence. They even had the killer ear-marked and he had selected the garrotte as his weapon of choice!"

"Phew! I would have been even more careful not to annoy him than ever I was if we had had any idea that John Scragg was into this sort of thing. What you have said makes them sound like terrorists."

"Terrorist: National Hero. It all depends whose side you are on. They themselves referred to their proposed work as 'scallywagging'!"

"How did all of this start and when?"

"So far as I can see, they were set up in mid-1940 as an initiative of Section D of the Secret Intelligence Service and were called GHQ Auxiliary Units. There were quite a few wartime bits and pieces with the tag 'Auxiliary' attached and so the name drew no attention to what they really were – the offspring of a SIS department specialising in what we now call terrorism. Then, later in 1940, Section D was passed to the Special Operations Executive by the SIS. From the very start, all of Section D's work was classified 'Most Secret' and that tag, now called 'Top Secret', technically still applies."

"But how were the Units set up using local people if it was all so secret?"

"It looks as though most were if fact recruited from the Local Defence Volunteers, or Home Guard as it was renamed. They were looking for active men in reserved occupations who could move about in the community without that being seen as odd and who knew the land very well. Obviously too, they wanted people who could keep their traps shut and who could rub along together under very stressful circumstances. The active patrol members were hand picked by the person recruited as the Unit leader. In one case, I believe, the whole patrol was from the same family. In the case of the Wiston Patrol, the leader was Jack Webley, father of the Webley brothers who were at school with you, who farmed Fairoak Farm at Wiston. The other five were John Heath who farmed at Muntham Farm near Findon, Burt Dean, a gamekeeper on the Wiston Estate, Jack Grange, the Land Agent to the Estate, Wilfred Howe who farmed close to Wiston and, of course, John Scragg."

"Interesting that a schoolmaster should be mixed up with what looks like a group of people from the local big estate plus a couple of nearby farmers."

"John would have known them all through a mixture of his shooting over the Wiston Estate and surrounding farms and his interest in local history which led him to explore the area thoroughly. He probably knew the lie of the land over a wide area better than any of the others. He also had experience of living in difficult conditions from his work in the Gold Coast which involved trekking through the bush to study outlying tribes."

"Who trained this bunch of locals and who told them to do what and when? You can't just pick a few people for the job you outlined and say 'OK chaps, off you go – and good luck'."

"In the specific case of the Wiston Patrol, I can't tell you. It is said that Jack Webley went off for special training and weekend courses were certainly laid on for the leaders and often others joined them. There is the possibility that some of this training was done at Windlesham House, near Washington, which was the local HQ for the Canadians. If it was, no-one would have remarked on unexpected absences because the trainees would not have had to spend a night away from home. The ones who got the special training were expected to pass their knowledge on to the rest. The courses were intensive and involved unarmed combat; use of hand weapons – coshes, garrottes, knives and so on; how to move silently and at night; how to set booby traps and carry out sabotage using the equipment provided; how to construct underground Operational Bases and arms dumps; how to use the firearms provided and so on. On the command side, each area – say the county of Sussex – would have had an Intelligence Officer who knew the Unit leaders and possibly the other members of each Unit. He was the person acting as a link between the Colonel in charge of the auxiliaries and the men on the ground. The whole idea was that as few people as possible knew who was who and where the Operational Bases were located. It was all very hush-hush! If auxiliaries had been in the Home Guard, all their documentation was withdrawn and destroyed. They became 'non-people' so far as the official records were concerned. This raised some problems initially with the police, who had grave doubts about auxiliaries found wandering about without authentication. After a couple of incidents, they were given slips of paper which said 'You must ask no questions of the Bearer, but telephone this number...' Not the thing to allay constabulary misgivings!!"

"What was their weaponry?"

"I thought you might ask that, Rodney, especially as you managed to find and use some of it! Actually, it was pretty basic at first. With the retreat of the British forces from continental Europe, their loss of equipment at Dunkirk was such that in re-arming the troops, nothing was left for anyone else. Still, Churchill was keen on the auxiliaries and both fair means and foul were used to find firearms. Someone had the bright idea of approaching the police to release some of the weapons handed in at the beginning of the war, only to find that the Home Office had ordered their destruction and dumping! The police in the USA were more forthcoming and many auxiliaries touted pistols marked 'New York Police'. Surprisingly quickly, though, special boxes of goodies were produced and issued to all Units. Want to see what you missed out on? I copied out the standard contents of the package supplied to each full Patrol of 7 people for you. It is quite impressive. The basic arms were:

7x .38-inch American revolvers; 2x .3-inch rifles; 7 fighting knives; 3 knobkerries; 48 No. 36 grenades with 4-second fuses; 3 cases No. 74 S.T. grenades; 2 cases No. 76 A.W. bottles; 1x .22-inch rifle with silencer, this was fitted with telescopic sights and was intended for sniping as well as shooting game to keep the Patrol in food when the rations ran out; 1 Thompson sub-machine gun later replaced by Sten guns. Plus 40x .38-inch pistol rounds; 200x .3-inch rifle rounds; 1000x .45 S.M.G rounds; 200x .22-inch rifle rounds.

To this you can add things such as garrottes, at first home-made, but later supplied. There was another grenade issued as standard, the No. 77 Smoke Grenade which used white phosphorus to create a smoke screen – the same sort of thing on a small scale as the controversial phosphorus shells used by the Israelis in Gaza. There were, of course all the explosives and associated triggers and fuses for use in sabotage. Significant is the fact that plastic explosive was issued to the Units. It is a highly effective and safe-to-use explosive which can be moulded into shape to do a pretty precise job. In fact I remember Johnny telling us how, after the war they used some PE to slice the top off a rookery, because the London hotels wanted rooks for 'game pie'! However, at that time it was supplied only through the SIS and, until the production of PE was sufficient to supply the Army too, it was issued through Section D almost exclusively to the Units."

"Yes, at least a couple of things there are familiar. I did pick up a packet of some explosive – not PE - but got scared and dumped it after one police search of the school failed to find it, but the AW bottles have to be what I call self-igniting phosphorus grenades –SIPs. I was out on a walk with a friend, Harry Hart, by Wiston Pond when we saw what looked like a couple of crates of ginger beer hidden in some reeds up at the shallow end, near the islands. Of course, we had to investigate and soon realised that they were more interesting than ginger beer! We got one bottle and took it with us back towards Mouse Lane where there were some large trees and threw it against one to see what would happen. There were flames and smoke everywhere. Next day, Harry went back to show someone else what we had found. Not wanting to incinerate another tree, he threw a bottle into the air and hit it with a thick branch as if he was serving a tennis ball. When the thing broke it splashed him pretty thoroughly and he burst into flames. Being beside the pond, he jumped in to extinguish himself. That was fine and well, but once phosphorus dries out it re-ignites. Anyway they set off running back to school, damping Harry down every so often from the Mouse Lane stream. Harry began to smoulder again as he rushed up the High Street. He asked me for help and we got him into a bath by Upper Dorm, clothes and all and sent for Matron. He was quite badly burned and the phosphorus burns took a long while to heal, but it could have been so much worse. Not a hope for his clothes, of course!"

"All the same, the thought of this frightened boy rushing through Steyning, streaming smoke behind him and vanishing into the main entrance to the school, does conjure up quite a picture!"

"All of this happened over the weekend and even better was that in the Monday Assembly the hymn chosen was 'As pants the hart for cooling streams when heated in the chase'. I'll take a small bet that that choice was Peter Woolf's. He played the piano if Captain Palmer-Stone didn't".

"Of course the cream of the jest can only now be appreciated: that some of his junior pupils had located one of John Scragg's ammo dumps and had not only done that, but had given the position away pretty comprehensively by using not just one but two grenades fairly publicly and because of the secrecy surrounding everything, he could not do much about it except, I suppose, to have chosen that hymn for Assembly if it wasn't Woolf's idea!"

"According to Colin Terry, it didn't end there either. As a known expert on explosives amongst the boys, he was asked to explain and demonstrate how the thing worked. They went up to the pond and the explanation was given. Three bottles were taken up to the Park wall by the main road and Colin hurled a couple of bottles against the wall, but with no immediate result. The third did the trick and there was an almighty bang and flames everywhere. No-one had noticed the herd of deer sitting minding its own business in the bracken by the wall. They now erupted in fright and quite a few leapt the wall and vanished into the surrounding countryside. Colin told me that local farmers were then issued with heavy game ammunition for their 12 bore shotguns so that they could shoot any they saw to protect the crops. No doubt a move highly appreciated by them with meat on the ration!"

"Colin went on to help produce the trigger for the UK's atom bomb, didn't he? Clearly SGS and explosives go together and big bangs from little SIPs grow!"

"I have no doubt that what Colin says is true enough, but it occurs to me that the farmers included at least three members of the Wiston Patrol and the story about being issued with special cartridges may well have been cover for the single slug cartridges several of the Units were given for their own shotguns early on when rifles etc were short. Those slugs were not widely available and would make a nasty hole in most things at fifty yards."

"Lucky for you perhaps, Rodney, that it was not a crate of No. 74 Sticky Bombs which you found!"

"What were they?"

"General opinion seems to be that they were designed by a sadistic madman! They looked a bit like the German stick grenades, but had a mixture of horrible and highly inflammable nasties inside on a five-second fuse. Round the head was a sock impregnated with a tremendously effective super-glue, protected by a casing which was removed before using the grenade. The idea was to fix the thing on to your target by throwing it or pressing it on and then, presumably, to run like hell. The problem, which John Warwicker points out in his excellent book, is that if you brushed the grenade against your trousers it stuck and you couldn't get it off. You then had to try to take off your boots, gaiters and trousers using one hand, whilst clinging grimly to the grenade and praying that you did not activate the fuse. All this, of course, in immediate proximity to the enemy and, with luck, at night! If you succeeded in your struggles, you then had to get back to base, trouser-less at the least and go through the hoops of getting another set of bags from some distant and disbelieving Quartermaster! In the meantime a puzzled enemy was worrying about the secret, self-igniting-trousers weapon blazing merrily nearby."

"You mentioned Operational Bases. Where was the Wiston one and what did they look like?"

"The first ones were pretty home made, but the later ones were quite well engineered and were often constructed by the Sappers to a basic design with a vertical entrance shaft into an underground chamber with room for seven men to sleep, feed and wash. There were rations to last two weeks – an indication of the life-expectancy of the Patrol should they go into action. Obviously, some arms were stored here, but there were other arms dumps round the Patrol's area – like the store which Rodney found with Harry Hart. There was, in fact, a recommendation that the SIPs should not be kept in the Base in case someone knocked one over and broke it. There was an emergency escape route from each Operational Base and it would certainly have been needed in a hurry if that had happened. The main problems seem to have been ventilation and damp, especially in the bases which the Patrols made themselves. The problem of damp was serious enough for the War Office to have an anti-condensation paint developed. Not ones to miss out on anything, they registered it with the Patent Office in 1940! Bases could be located anywhere and the entries might be from under latrines in barns or other spots inside buildings used by people or stock, but for the Auxiliary Units, as opposed to some of the other clandestine groups operating in the same secretive ways, they were usually in woods or other wild places, into and out of which men could ghost at night. The Wiston Patrol is said to have had its Base in a spinney below Chanctonbury Ring, but it has never been located. My personal guess is that it is somewhere in Copyhold Wood, because that is on an outcrop of the Folkestone Sand. This is easy to dig into; can hold unsupported tunnels at a pinch; and, above all, is well drained. Digging into the chalk of the Downs is harder work; you have fresh chalk to get rid of; and chalk is an aquifer and liable to leak on you! The Wiston Patrol is said to have had a major arms dump constructed in the chalk above Coombes Farm, but that was dug in an existing chalk pit where fresh chalk would not be noticed. Below the chalk is Upper Greensand, which is harder still and which throws springs out all along the base of the Downs. No, a Folkestone Sand woodland sounds right to me. There would be lookout posts too, connected by telephone to the Base, to warn of approaching friends, foes or inquisitive schoolboys! In fact, I expect that this particular wood was rarely entered by the boys. Certainly in my time no-one went there and the natives were not very friendly!"

"Sounds a bit cramped and uncomfortable and would have been awful with any operational stress. I suppose that someone had to get out to select targets and so on."

"Yes, I believe that the idea was for the lookout to prospect the target for the night strike. It was general practice too to leave guns behind because the whole idea was silence and stealth. Fire-fights were not to be encouraged except as the last resort."

"I was told about the making of one of these bases," Rodney exclaimed, "It was done by Canadian Sappers, because they didn't know the ground and so could not give the location away. It was in the basement of a pub near Arundel and all other than the landlord were excluded from the area while the Sappers dug down and tunnelled under the main road into the grounds of a convent. Under a tree they constructed a chamber to hold a wireless operator and ran an aerial up the tree in a slim channel cut into the bark. The pub end entrance was camouflaged and the landlord sworn to secrecy. It was all filled in after the war."

"That is a spot-on description of quite another and even more secret Auxiliary Unit than the one to which John Scragg belonged," I told him, "The radio operator was linked to places such as Bletchley Park and passed on messages from listeners to the enemy signals for information or for decoding. The entrances to the operators' hidey-holes were invariably in buildings and these bases catered for one person. The Special Units' bases were always out in the countryside and were for 6-7 people. Communication between messengers and the operator could be like something out of an adventure comic! In one case, agents left messages in a telegraph pole which had a cavity hollowed out behind a metal label. When a message had been left, the label was turned to face upside-down. A runner on observing this would extract the message and take it to where a split tennis ball was placed in a derelict playground and into it messages were pushed. The ball was taken to a tree stump and this, if you knew how, could be swivelled to expose a tube down which the ball was dropped. It then fell into an inclined pipe which ran for a considerable distance before dropping the ball out on to the operator's desk."

"Interesting, but I bet that the authorities were pretty anxious that no word got out about anything like this to compromise operations. It seems somehow all a bit in the public eye to me."

"That reminds me of something else! Each Patrol of the Special Units had a gallon of rum to be opened only to relieve pain of injury or when capture was inevitable. The idea was that if well rummed-up, an auxiliary could withstand interrogation for longer. In 1944 when the Units were disbanded, the War Department demanded the return of this rum with the seals intact. Auxiliaries had been selected for their initiative and it is said that many of the returned containers with 'intact' seals held green tea – or something looking similar to it!"

"That does not surprise me at all!"

"Well, although keen to recover the rum, the authorities seemed less concerned about other things. One Group Leader, having waited twenty years for someone to come collect the spare armaments he was holding, broke the vow of secrecy to the extent of informing the police. His cowshed held, according to Warwicker's book: 14,748 rounds of ammunition; 1,205 lbs of explosives; 3,742 feet of delayed action fuse; 930 feet of safety fuse; 144 time pencils; 1,207 L-delay switches; 1,271 detonators; 719 booby-trap switches; 314 paraffin bombs; 121 smoke bombs; 36 slabs of guncotton and 33 time pencils and booby-trap switches attached to made up charges. A few pounds of explosives can destroy a major building and this group had over half a ton!"

"Enough to start a young war!"

"I'm still a bit puzzled though about the secrecy side of things. They seem to have blown hot and cold and at one time I remember that John showed some people the Fairbairn-Sykes Commando knife he was issued with and explaining how plastic explosive could be moulded to give precision results."

"Ah, that was due to changes in command. The first phase emphasised total secrecy and independent working of each Patrol. They had a general instruction about what to do, but were expected to use their initiative, their local knowledge and training in the case of invasion. The next commander was a Regular and wanted things put on a more normal Army-style footing. This was when the auxiliaries were affiliated to the Home Guards – although there was no paperwork covering this and the auxiliaries remained 'non-people' - and were supposed to appear on church parades and things like that. It was felt that this would screen them from criticism as shirkers and help to explain their nocturnal comings and goings. They were also organised into larger Groups with the idea that they could channel numbers into one area under a Group Commander. This ran contrary to the whole concept of the Auxiliary Units acting independently over ground which they knew intimately and compromised security. With the next change in command, it was back to high secrecy again."

"Normal shambles! But it explains the occasional appearance of John in Home Guard uniform."

"I suppose that the secrecy was kept up for so long because it would be a bit embarrassing politically to admit that the Government had trained up a clandestine force under the direction of the Secret Services rather than the normal military Command and that one objective was to eliminate people thought to be a threat to the Government's war time plans. That could easily tip over into peacetime!"

"I take your point and suspect that there is truth in it, but I think that the auxiliaries were a small unit caught up in a much broader web of secret units and deceit, elements of which still operate and that is why the cloak of secrecy is still there."

"All very sobering stuff and to think that it was there under our noses and that we did better on one occasion than I hope that the Germans would have done in finding the arms dumps!"

"Rodney, you don't know whether or not someone with a familiar face was watching you at your moment of discovery through the telescopic sights of a .22 sniper's rifle. If it was, the temptation must have been great!"

Pre-war trip to the beach at Lancing

Eating buns after swimming on a pre-war trip to the beach at Lancing.

'Razzo' Ross on the Playing Field. Late 1930s.

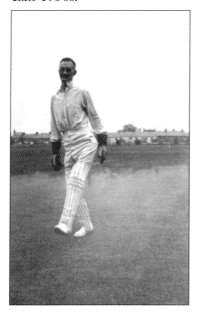

Mr Barnes with junior boys on the Playing Field. Mid-1930s.

Scouts building a bridge across the tail of Court Mill Pond. 1941.

Gymnastics 1940

Cricket Team on the Playing Field. Early 1940s. Chanctonbury Ring can be seen in the far distance.

The funeral of five German airmen killed when their plane crashed in 1941.

A sketch by 17-year-old John Grantham of the train being machine-gunned in 1942 near West Grinstead station.

Old Malthouse Cottages in the 1930s. They were about 40 years old when destroyed in 1943.

Salvaging belongings from the rubble shortly after the bomb fell on the Old Malthouse Cottages.

After the rubble had been cleared showing the wide area damaged. Chantry Green House is to the left of the photo.

From
THE HEADMASTER.
Tel. Steyning 3153.

THE GRAMMAR SCHOOL,
STEYNING,
SUSSEX.

26th March, 1943.

Dear Mr. Still,

Thank you for your letter.

I have tried to find any boys who are travelling in Anthony's direction next Wednesday, but unfortunately no boy is going further than Horsham.

I will undertake to see that he is escorted to Horsham on the train leaving Steyning at 12.36 and arriving at Horsham at 1.14. I understand that there is another train leaving Horsham at 1.48 which reaches Three Bridges at 2.5.

I will arrange for his ticket to be booked through to Headcorn and his trunk sent Passenger Luggage in advance.

Yours sincerely,

W. H. Still, Esq.,
Kingsworth Manor,
ULCOMBE,
Kent.

Trying to get a young boy safely home after term in 1943.

Receipt for a term's fees for a boarder in 1943.

STEYNING GRAMMAR SCHOOL.

Parent or Guardian W. Still Esq.,
Autumn Term, 19 43

No. 194

Boy's Name
Still
a.

Amount Paid

Received on behalf of the Governors of Steyning Grammar School the sum specified hereon as '......' this 20th day of September 1943

Lloyds Bank Limited, Steyning. £ 24 18 0

		£	s	d	
A. FEES for above Term payable in advance:	TUITION (including stationery)	5	5	–	01
	BOARDING	16	16	–	02
	DINNERS				03
	PIANOFORTE				04
	MEDICAL ATTENDANCE		8	5	05
	INSURANCE		12	–	06
	SEA BATHING				07
	SCOUTS or CUBS				08
	ARREARS				09
B. SUNDRIES for the previous Term: (Bills enclosed)	SCHOOL OUTFITTER		5	11	10
	BOOT REPAIRS				11
	CHEMIST		1	9	12
					13
OTHER SUNDRIES for the previous Term:	EXTRA DINNERS				14
	SICK ROOM		10	–	15
	MATRON'S ACCOUNT		1	–	16
	EXTRA LAUNDRY				17
	DRY CLEANING				18
	HAIRDRESSER		7		19
	POCKET MONEY		6	6	20
	X CASH ADVANCED			3	21
	LUGGAGE		1	10	22
	BOOKS or MUSIC SUPPLIED				23
	PRIVATE TUITION				24
	WORKSHOP MATERIALS				25
	MILK		1	10	26
	A.R.P. 6/- Bus fare 1/6		7	6	13
	This Account must be paid not later than the First Day of the Term. £	24	18	9	

stamps

The School Term begins at 9 a.m. on 21 SEP 1943
Boarders return not later than 7 p.m. on the previous day.
A pupil is liable to be refused admission unless the Fees have been paid.
A term's notice is required to be given in writing of the intention to remove a pupil, otherwise a term's fees must be paid.

This form in its entirety, accompanied by the fees, must be forwarded to :
The Manager, Lloyds Bank Ltd., Steyning, or handed in at any Branch of that Bank.
Cheques should be made payable to Lloyds Bank Ltd.

Left to right. Seated: Stanley Bayliss Smith, John Scragg. Cross-legged: Peter Flateau, John Norman, Malcolm Swann. May 1940.

Wiggonholt Church where John Norman's ashes are buried.

69

Old Boys from 1943 and Ian Norman's family by John Norman's memorial stone. 8 March 2004.

Geoffrey Mason competing in the long jump on Sports Day 1943. Note Mr Bennett's fine example of a 'short back and sides' haircut!

School Cadets at the 1945 Cadet Camp. C.S.M. Leo Cruttenden on the far left

Chantry Green House decorated after VE Day by the Engineering Group of the 43rd Royal Marine Commandos.

Scout Camp at Corfe in 1946. Chris Passmore and Noel Moloney playing deck quoits with David Broomfield watching.

Twelfth Night, 1946. 'Put up your swords!'

Chris Passmore as Maria in Twelfth Night in 1946. He got a special award for the best female impersonation.

Holland House (boarders) outside the Headmaster's study. June 1947. The Masters are (l-r) Idris David, John Scragg and Bill Lewis.

'Barrel' Clover in the playground with Form 2A. Spring 1947. Air-raid shelter to the left.

Freda Sage arranging the 1947 Art Exhibition in the gymnasium.

Elsie and Doris Waters (Gert and Daisy) with a group of boys at the 1947 Art Exhibition.

STEYNING GRAMMAR SCHOOL.

Scout Camp 1948

Address   The Camp address will be:-

                    2nd Steyning Troop,
                    New House Farm,
                    EAST DEAN,
                    Chichester, Sussex.

The site is ¾ of a mile north of East Dean and is approached from village by main road sign posted "Farm and Downs only". There is a bus service from Chichester to East Dean.

Visitors' Day   Visitors will be welcome and the Troop will remain in camp to receive them on the afternoon of Sunday, May the 16th.

Cost   The cost of the camp will be £1.10.0. This should be paid to me by Tuesday, May the 4th.

Travel   The Troop will depart straight from School on Friday May the 14th and return to Steyning at about 3.30 p.m. on May the 21st. The journey will be made by coach.

Rules   The Boy Scouts Association requires the following rules to be observed:-
1) Uniform will be worn outside camp boundaries. No Scout should go outside these boundaries without leave from the Scoutmaster.
2) Care must be taken not to damage crops, hedges &c. and all gates must be kept shut.

Personal Gear   Each Scout will require the following items, which should be clearly marked with his name. Gear to be carried should be packed in a rucksack or kitbag.

Complete Scout Uniform.	Sweater.
3 Blankets (or Sleeping Bag.)	Spare Boots or Shoes.
Pyjamas or change for night.	Plimsolls or sandals.
Spare shirt, shorts & stockings.	Bathing suit.
Soap, Comb, brush, toothbrush &c.	Towel.
in toilet bag.	
Handkerchiefs.	Groundsheet (and/or Mackintosh.)
Knife, fork, spoon, enamelled mug.	Ration Book & Identity Card.

Food Coupons   A food permit will be obtained for the period of the camp. It is essential that all Ration Books should contain coupons, points and B.U's for the 4th week of Period 11. Only these will be used.

                                    W.H.LEWIS.
                                    Scoutmaster.

Arrangements for a Scout Camp in 1948.

DATE	NAME	OFFENCE	PUNISHMENT	SIGNATURE	DUE BY.
28th Nov	Pepys [initials]	Gr. Insolence	By Hurst	F. West Gd	Wednesday 10.35
20th/11th.	Morris	Previous punishment not done	8 sides	R. Maitgard.	Thursday 10. 35.
28.11.49	Allan	Talking in Prep	2 sides c.P	P.Stew;	Thursday 6.30
"	Hewitt	" "	2 sides c.P	P.Stew;	Thursday 6.30
"	Rountree	Previous punishment not done and running in corridor after prep	4 sides c.P	P.Stew;	Thursday 6.30
	Isama			P.Stew;	Thursday 6.30
30th	Pepys (?)	Talking in dormitory	1 sides	F. West Gd	Wednesday 5.30
30 /11th.	Vallance	Knocking a chair and by default, 3 yrs a chair for 2	2 sides	R. Maitgard.	Thursday Break.
1st Dec.	Morris	Punishment not attempted for second time	Reported to Head.	C.F. Maitgard.	✓
1st Dec.	Mckenzie	Incident	1 hr. Detention	Lot Fog	✓
1st Dec.	Upton	Eating on Station	1. Detention	Lot Fog	✓
1st Dec	James	Continual talking in	Pipers ?	Lot Fog	✓
Dec 1	Taylor	Bullying	Lines to do	W.P.T. McVaney	✓
Dec 1	Taylor	Destructive	otherl - meals	2 W.P.T. McVaney	✓
Dec 2.	Holden	Sliding down Banisters	2 sides c.P	P.Stew;	Saturday 12.
Dec 2.	Elborough	2 Previous Punishments Not Completed	Detention	D.D. White	Dec 3. 5.05.
Dec 2.	Bacon (2.m)	Eating and dropping sweets Catriotes	2 slides on Prep.	R. Maitgard.	Dec 4th. Break.
Dec 4th	Joyce	Using Porters Entrance to Blue P.C	prev by fawet D.T.	Purnell	

Pages from the House Prefects' Punishment Book, Christmas Term 1949. The book was inspected and initialled periodically by the Headmaster. John Scragg's initials appear here against the first name on the page.

The 1950 Founder's Day procession to the church, led by 'Spud' Crannigan, followed by Doug Harvey, two of the post-war recruits to the staff.

Wisden Stenning in 1933. Killed in action 1941.

CHAPTER 6

Enemy in sight

Steyning never was a target of any significance during the war. Once the threat of invasion had receded and with one possible exception, attack from the air was confined to a handful of opportunistic, almost incidental, events. When late in the war, the D-Day build-up of troops and armaments gave more reason for concentrated attack, the RAF had become dominant and in any case targets on offer in the town were insignificant when compared with those nearer the south coast ports. Day boys were more familiar with air raids than the boarders, especially where they came from places such as Shoreham. While this insulation encouraged a detached attitude in the boys to the progress of the war, it in no way discouraged them from extracting the last ounce of excitement and drama from what did go on. One boy's diary bemoans the fact that he was not on the scene when a Heinkel machine-gunned the High Street. He did, however, draw comfort by going to Duke's timber yard to inspect some planks which had borne the brunt of this savage attack.

The Battle of Britain was followed avidly as planes wheeled and swooped and souvenirs were sought and swapped in the form of spent cartridges, shrapnel, bits of aircraft and anything else of the faintest connection with hostilities. Many boys could out-perform the Observer Corps in aircraft identification and those who could get to Shoreham airport were eager plane-spotters. John Scragg had once noticed an aircraft new to him. It was identified immediately from his description as a Buccaneer by a boy, and he was amused by the comment: 'You lucky thing, sir! But you didn't know what it was and that's no good!'

The relative peace and quiet in Steyning ensured that when something did happen, everyone remembers it. Everyone, that is, remembers a version of events differing in detail or in substance from that recalled by everyone else. This complication does not crop up where the action took place away from the town, for example, when a bomb scored a direct hit on the Hiscock's herd of cows in the Steyning Bowl, close to Upper Maudlin Farm. Ken Hiscock remembers it vividly and with a sorrow which his school friends cannot share.

Ken also experienced one very odd event. He and a friend were walking over the Downs less than quarter of a mile from Ken's farm when they came across a Lysander aircraft on the ground with two men beside it. The men got in hastily and the aircraft took off, to the boys' regret. Regret turned into terror when the plane swung back and swooped on them, doing so several times before flying off. When the two frightened boys told Ken's father, he contacted the officer in charge of the machine-gun post which had been set up on nearby Steep Down to complain. He was told that no Lysanders were flying in the area since all were grounded. One had been captured in the retreat of the BEF from France. It was thought it was being used by the Germans for reconnaissance along the south coast and everyone had orders to shoot down any Lysander found over Sussex.

Although they missed this one, the RAF and local anti-aircraft batteries brought down other aircraft in the vicinity of Steyning and landed damaged aircraft of their own. Shoreham Airport was used frequently to land damaged planes, including large ones such as Flying Fortress, all of which interested the boys as they passed by.

"It must have been about here that the plane came down and burned. That Press report said 400 yards down the track leading from between Lower and Upper Wyckham to Scotland Farm. It came in from the direction of the Devil's Dyke and fire broke out on board when it was over Kings Barn Farm and it didn't get far after that. Its cargo of incendiary bombs burned for a good four hours until well gone midnight."

"I assume that the crew died?"

"Yes, all five of them. I've got the list of names from the Museum: Graf Zu Castell, Guenther Jansom, Heinz Schubert, FK Zaver Kroiss and Guenther Lenning. They were buried in two graves in Steyning churchyard and the bodies repatriated after the war."

"Why two graves?"

"No idea. Sorry! Could have been officers and ORs, I suppose. Whatever, there was a bit of a row about it all when a member of the British Legion wrote to the local paper saying that they should not be buried in the churchyard. This was taken up in the National Press and the local British Legion then wrote to dissociate itself from the original writer – who was not a local member. The vicar, Mr Cox, then simply rolled over the opposition by saying 'we should deal graciously with them' and the deed was done!"

"I remember that Kitchener told me that he saw the thing as it flew over Small Dole. I had forgotten that his family had moved there briefly before he became a boarder. He said that he heard this great roaring noise over the house and saw a vast silhouette moving above him like some visitor from outer space."

"Pretty dramatic stuff!"

"Well, we didn't get much happening like that near the school. Down on the coast it was not too bad either, but there was a good deal more action there."

A group of four of us was meandering along having strolled out of Steyning to try to settle a discussion about a Heinkel 111 bomber which had crashed in January 1941. The party was now directing its rather aged and weary feet towards one of the pleasant oases still on offer in Steyning, but bemoaning the loss from these watering holes of the Soldier's Return, the Railway Inn, the George and the Three Tuns – to say nothing of the Brewer's Arms which had, before the time of any of us, been an integral part of what we knew as the school. It was bought by the school from the Steyning Brewery in 1908 to be converted into offices. Its presence would have been off-set so far as teachers were concerned by the noisy activities of the cooper working in No. 7 and the blacksmith opposite Holland Cottage, to say nothing of the alcoholic musings coming from the bar itself! Since the Norfolk Arms was by a hundred yards or so the nearest to us as we walked back along Kings Barn Lane, it was here that we settled to look at maps.

"Right! We have that one pretty well fixed. What about any others?"

"Were there any others?"

"No bombers like the Wyckham Heinkel so close to the town, although early in the war, another came down, crippled by a Hurricane, at the back of the Round Hill near Maudlin Barn. As it came down, the upper gunner fired at the army camp up there and the fire was returned, wounding him fatally. The plane made a belly-landing and was largely intact. Ken Hiscock and his dad went up with their shot guns and although there were a lot of soldiers around, Ken's dad was put in charge of the prisoners. Ken reckons that they more impressed by his dad with his 12 bore than with a fourteen-year-old holding a 4.10! The Germans were not particularly sympathetic to their dying comrade, one saying 'That fool! No-one was hurt until he started shooting at your Tommies'. The Bomb Disposal bods destroyed the bomb load and the plane was put under guard – not that it stopped us going to have a good look!"

"I heard that a Messerschmidt 110 was shot down in Steyning itself. Is that true?"

"Indeed it is! It was quite interesting, although I only had it all at second or third hand. Apparently, it was being chased by one of our fighters and had been damaged. The pilot made as if to land on the Playing Field, but then realised that he would crash into houses along Newham Lane because there was not enough room to get down safely. As he opened up to vault the houses, our pilot thought that he was making a break for it and fired, rattling a lot of roof tiles and bringing it down in a potato field near Duke's timber yard. The rear gunner was dead. The pilot was more or less OK, but very young and crying bitterly and the soldiers escorting him to the police station spent most of their time warding off the vindictive townsfolk. One old gent, not content with giving verbal abuse, kept trying to kick the boy."

"What with that and the row about the graveyard, it makes you wonder a bit about the locals. Still, it was wartime and people were scared of invasion; had little idea about what was actually going on; and believed what the papers said. As usual, the media were at the bottom of a lot of the poorly-informed hatred surrounding things like internment. You can't blame folk for doing things they would not have dreamt of doing in peacetime. Anyway, I guess it would only be a few – again as usual – who were so extreme."

"I was told that the guns from the nose of the plane were taken to Wiston House and mounted on the lawn. They called it the Brigadier's Baby and even managed to knock some bits off a damaged plane with the thing as it flew over."

"Do you know, that was really about it so far as aircraft being downed close to Steyning are concerned. Over towards the coast there were more, both British and German and there were more or less random events elsewhere which individual boys experienced. Wright told me about a bomber which crashed near Billingshurst in 1941 and how he had picked up a flying glove, but threw it away when he realised it still had a hand inside it."

"Interesting that, because I have heard the same thing about other crashes – the Heinkel we went to look for just now, for example. There were either a lot of hand-filled gloves lying around, or it is a case of an urban myth!"

"The Webleys over at Wiston said that a couple of Spitfires had crashed not far from their farm and that they had a cow injured by a bomb. A German aircraft shot at one of them when he was out riding, but none of this is up to London blitz standards. We were very lucky!"

"All the same, day boys in particular could be given unpleasant greetings from Germany from time to time and most from the coast were conditioned to ducking under desks as soon as a low-flying plane was heard. You could tell the boys who lived inland because they were the ones still sitting in their places! We spent little time in the air raid shelters – once we eventually got them – but I was told that Portslade Primary School spent an average of ten hours a week in shelters and the same would have been true of most schools in that area."

"You had to watch out for planes going back to Germany because they had a habit of flying low and machine-gunning any town or village they passed over. You often got little or no warning. I was going to school from Southwick when the street I was going down got shot up by a Heinkel. I dived behind a wall as bullets pattered all around, but got to school on time, which seemed more important to me then than nearly having been shot!"

"Yes, Don Shearer and his mother had a similar experience in Steyning when the High Street got sprayed. They dodged into a shop doorway."

"There was just one fatal shooting which I heard of, but that was at West Grinstead when the Steyning Flyer was shot up and the driver, George Ansbridge, was killed. Johnnie Grantham did a rather good sketch of the attack which he had seen."

"The incoming air fleets didn't give us a lot of concern since they had their targets mostly in London. Brian Oddy told me that at least 100 German aircraft flew over as he was walking to Bramber and it never occurred to him to take cover. You just kept on walking."

"The Battle of Britain was a case apart, wasn't it? We took every chance to get out and watch and it was remote enough for the most part to be like watching a film or a football match. Planes got cheered (ours) and booed (theirs) and the fact that people were being killed seemed almost irrelevant."

"I take your point, but I did get a rude awakening once. I was up on Flagstaff Hill when I noticed a splendid dog-fight and stayed to watch, but suddenly bullets began to slam into the ground around me. I got really scared and dived into a ditch for cover. Quite a bit later a prefect, Peter Woolf, was sent up to rescue me and bring me back to school."

"I can almost hear John Scragg saying ' Woolf, go up Flagstaff Hill; tell them to stop the war for five minutes; get that wretched boy down here; and tell him to stand outside my study.'"

"Luckily, this was before he was Head and because I was a boarder, he wasn't my Housemaster either!"

"There was one interesting event brought on by air raids and which I have only heard mentioned by a few of whom would have been the senior boys of the time. That is that, after registration, the School Register was taken over to Dog Lane and lodged in the ARP base. This was in case the school was hit. There needed to be an accurate record of who was in the buildings. I'm unsure whether there was a duplicate register kept in the school itself."

"There were lots of odd stories going around explaining strange things which we noticed. Does anyone else remember going cross-country running one morning and finding the whole countryside full of spiders' webs? We speculated that the Germans had developed some carrier looking like webs to use in germ warfare. At least our imaginations were fertile!"

"I can't say that I recall that, but I do remember those spirals of tinsel falling from the sky. I think that both sides used this ploy to confuse the radar, but it was as if every day was Christmas!"

"What did the Government say to explain things like this? It can't have been just schoolboys who had daft ideas and started rumours."

"Well, I know from my mother's experience that you believed the official line at your peril! When the first V2 landed in Chiswick, the official line was that a gas main had exploded. Of course, everyone living in the area knew that this was untrue!"

"I suppose that the officials had to try to defuse situations which could have led to panic. They could certainly come out with very reassuring advice – reassuring, that is, until you thought the thing through! How about those invasion posters on how to stop a German tank? The answer was to walk casually alongside it carrying a blanket, as one normally did of course, and feed the blanket into the tracks, thereby jamming them. One has a vision of a gent dressed in a suit, carrying a furled umbrella and a copy of *The Times*, wearing a bowler and with a blanket folded neatly over his arm, saying a cheerful 'Good morning' to a baffled German tank commander as he fed the blanket into the tracks. 'Got to keep the tracks warm, old chap!'"

"There was another good one about stopping a German soldier from raping you. You poked his eyes out and kneed him in the balls. Very sensible, but a bit easier said than done – and what about the rest of the sexually frustrated and rampant horde even now advancing towards you across the mud and shingle of the beaches of Lancing and Shoreham?"

"There definitely was an air of total unreality to all of this, you know. Certainly, as schoolboys, we were semi-detached from what was actually happening. Probably just as well, although I have a suspicion that it was some kind of instinctive defence mechanism too."

"As Pooh Bear said, *'I am a Bear of Very Little Brain, and long words Bother me'*. May I interpolate a sentence of short words and of commendable brevity? 'It is your round'."

CHAPTER 7

Was it Riedel?

"*A*t 12.22 a FW 190 came over very low and 3 seconds later there was a terrific crash. We dived under our desks. Then went to Shelter 3. I saw a bloody soldier being carried through the streets. The lock was blown off the front door and various windows broken. The bomb was less than 50 yards away* [in fact it fell over 100 yards from the school classrooms]. *4 cottages, one man and woman and part of Eaton's sweet shop. Beeding machine-gunned at 12.40 and cow killed.*"

This was 13-year-old Tony Randle's diary entry for Thursday 18 February 1943. It describes succinctly one of the most abiding memories of the school during the war and one which, since everyone in the school at the time experienced it, contains in these memories a number of apparently contradictory statements as the passage of time has rounded off corners and compressed sequences.

It also embodies a school myth that the bomb was dropped by one of the Riedel brothers, whose ambition on leaving school was to join the Luftwaffe and who had promised to come back with a bomb. There is no doubt that this promise was made, but the Riedels had enjoyed their time at Steyning in the late 1930s and were quite popular with other boys. It seems to have been no more than a schoolboy joke – and one received with acclamation by the juniors of his day! It might equally have been made by a boy leaving to join the RAF's Bomber Command and with no greater seriousness. However, the Riedels were very pro-Hitler, for all his faults, (just as later on in Steyning, schoolboys were pro-Churchill with all of his faults) and a year after they returned to Germany, we were at war.

After the elapse of over 65 years we are faced with authoritative accounts of a Messerschmidt 109/ Messerschmidt 110/ Focke-Wulf 190/Heinkel 111 attacking the school/Chantry Green House from the northwest/southeast/east with one/two bombs and with the face of one of the Riedels clearly visible as the plane climbed away! I leave aside discrepancies in the account of the damage caused. Suffice to say that they are considerable, but mainly over matters of detail.

If the various accounts are looked at in isolation, chaos reigns. Taken as a whole, it is possible to tease out an account which is plausible and which can make sense of what at first sight seem contradictory stories. Chris Tod, Curator of Steyning Museum, has been caught in the cross-fire of these recollections and what has been in effect a committee of enquiry consisting of Geoffrey Mason, Rodney Cox and myself has been sifting the evidence to give a clearer picture of what actually happened, as well as to suggest what might also have happened. In 1943, Geoffrey was Head Boy and Rodney a 13-year-old boarder. I was two-and-a-half years old and so brought no personal memories to the table, but a mass of written material collected from assorted Old Boys and other sources over a nine year period.

The three of us were taking our ease over a cup of tea and some cakes in the lounge at Springwells. A large box file of letters and other documents sat on the table and was being eyed reluctantly by us all. At length someone said that we had better get down to work. Geoffrey then showed the talent of a true Staff Officer by remarking that since I had read all of the papers in detail, perhaps I would give a synopsis and he and Rodney would throw spanners into my works as the occasion demanded.

"What we need to establish first are the facts." he said, "What do we know to be true? We can then look as needs be at the more ornamental details. Can we start with the date and the plane? Was it definitely the 18th of February 1943 at around half-past twelve in the morning? And can we settle on the plane being a FW 190?"

"Yes, I am quite sure that we can agree there," I answered with confidence, "The majority of witnesses and the Press reports all say a FW 190 and the date and time are safe although another contemporary diary gives the time as 'exactly 12.35' instead of 12.22 and an account in the Museum suggests 12.45. I am equally certain that only one bomb was dropped and the official account that it was a 500lb one sounds reasonable in view of the damage caused. We can also be sure that it was the Old Malthouse Cottages which bore the brunt of the explosion."

"So far, so good! But now we come to a more difficult question and one quite relevant to whether the attack was aimed at the school or not – what was the plane's line of attack? Was its bombing run from the direction of Chanctonbury Ring or from the general direction of the Round Hill? My own clear memory is of watching the plane climb away more or less over the trees in Coombe Court garden. That would not be possible if he came in from the Round Hill and flew over the school, but boys in Razzo Ross's class in Room 7 saw the plane flying more or less straight at them, which can only mean an approach from the Round Hill/Adur valley."

"That conundrum is a bit like a classic detective story. It all revolves round personal character and timing! Razzo was a stubborn old soul and saw little reason why the sodding great crash of a bomb, the broken glass in windows and a general pall of dust should disturb his French lesson. The accounts say that he banged his desk hard with his stick, told them all to sit down and asked poor Van Tromp to go on reciting irregular French verbs thus: *'Asseyez vous!! Continuez Guillaume'*. This took a few moments before he had to reprimand someone for pointing out, in English rather than in French, that a German aircraft was closing rapidly on the classroom windows. At this point and only then, did he suggest that the class should now join the rest of the school in the air raid shelters. In the meantime, Stanley Bayliss Smith in the Art Room, the other side of Upper Corridor to Room 7, having calmly watched the plane climb away as Geoffrey describes it, told his class to go down the fire escape at the end of the building and into the air raid shelter at the bottom of it. When halfway down the fire escape, Doug Pennifold saw the plane heading straight for them from the general direction of the Round Hill and was terrified of being machine-gunned. It flew over without firing and then veered away, presumably to go back to Germany, having inspected the damage caused by the bomb. It was this inspection flight which Razzo's class had seen. Draw a straight line from the bog to Chantry Green House and extend it back towards the Downs and you have the track. The attack was from the Chanctonbury direction, possibly using the main road as the guide line from Wiston Park."

"This casts doubt on the idea that the attack was an opportunistic one on the school by an aircraft looking for any old target before going home! I never believed that. When I plotted the line of attack, I all but knew for sure that the target had been Chantry Green House. He only missed by a few yards, for heavens sake!"

"To be honest, Rodney, this has all the hall-marks of an Intelligence-led, targeted attack, not on the school, which had no military significance, but on a nearby target of some importance, as you rightly suggest. The plane came in low along a carefully plotted route with excellent guidelines on the ground. If you get a ruler and draw a line from Staplefields to Coombe Court, you have the probable attack run. It bombed from about 100 feet. The buildings actually hit were 100 yards from the nearest bit of the school and more like 150 yards from the classrooms. To miss a target by that much from 100 feet would have been quite a difficult job in itself, even if the attack had come from the Round Hill direction where the plane flew over the school! The pilot came back to look at the result, not something done when a target is a random one. I am discounting here the one account from an evacuee staying at Fletchers Croft, that the plane had come in from east to west, turning on its wingtips to pass between two trees. There are just too many eye-witnesses who say it was a west to east attack. His account, if accurate, sounds more like one of our lot showing off! From all that we know from the accounts of others and from what you both recall, I would bet, as you do, that the target was Chantry Green House where the Royal Marines frogmen were based at the time. It also housed the Home Guards and was a good target because of that, but especially so given the presence of the Commandos."

"I take your reasoning, George, but would like to get confirmation that the Commandos were there in 1943. They were certainly there in 1944, but I am not sure just when they arrived. They were a quiet bunch of people – as is usually the case amongst special troops."

"That I can't give you, I'm afraid, although Hollins gives it as a reason why the House might have been targeted. He lived in Gordon House on the opposite side of Church Street to the school and so was close to what went on there. The information may surface later, but it hasn't yet!"

"I didn't realise that Hollins lived there. Gordon House was where Parnell was married to Kitty O'Shea in 1891, the year that he died!"

"Well, I don't think that Irish republicanism had anything to do with this bomb! However, I can offer you a bit more evidence about how close the strike was to Chantry Green House. Bob Miller lived in Highland Croft and was friends of the Cummings family who lived in the Old Malthouse Cottages. He talked to an officer who had been in conversation with another Home Guard officer in the doorway to Chantry House. He was sheltered somehow from the blast itself, but seconds before the explosion, saw the bomb bounce off the surface of Church Street and in through the window of the Cummings's front room. That brings the miss on Chantry Green House down to a matter of some 60 feet in a line on the ground. If you remember your geometry, if a bomb is dropped from 100 feet by an aircraft travelling at, say, 200mph at a building standing around 35 feet tall and misses the base of the building by 60 feet, it hasn't missed the top of the building by more than inches. A very near thing, in fact."

"I suppose that there was a short delay set on the detonator to allow the plane to climb away before the bomb went off and that this allowed the bomb to bounce off the road before exploding."

"Pretty certain, I'd say."

"Given that it was an attack targeted on Chantry Green House, why didn't they come back when the mission failed?"

"I can only suggest that either they thought that the raid had been successful – the surrounding buildings were indeed damaged and some quite badly, as well as the cottages and there was a lot of dust and smoke when the pilot came back to take a look – or that the target was not thought of sufficiently high priority to warrant a second strike. The first would have rung alarm bells too and they may have thought that the target would be better defended second time round."

"That sounds reasonable to me. I expect too that there were people rushing about all over the place, adding to the sense of confusion on the ground."

"From what you mentioned on the phone, I understand that there is a good measure of agreement about the reaction in the school to the blast."

"That's right. The first comment by most is that everyone dived under desks, or at least dived to the floor. An exception was John Sennitt who found himself the only one in the class left sitting in his place. He was one of the people who lived away from the coast on the edge of Storrington and was not acclimatised to sporadic bombing. The rest hit the deck! There is repeated reference to the calm and authority of the staff. Razzo took it to extremes, perhaps, but the rest simply told people to get up and walk to the shelters. The next general impressions were of dust. There was the smell of that dislodged from the classrooms themselves, but then also the sight of a dense cloud of dust and smoke rising from the ruins. Moore and Waine both mention a mass of feathers floating in the dust cloud and assume, probably rightly, that these came from furnishings such as pillows and eiderdowns rather than from live chickens. Both Shearer and Wells talk about sparkling fragments in the air and although Don Shearer put this down to fragments of glass, I think that Wells's opinion that these were particles of straw from the thatch is correct, especially since the air remained 'sparkly' for quite a time. Later common recollections include clothes hanging from the trees on Chantry Green. These stayed there for months before rotting away. There was also the case of the human leg which some had seen in the road. This was Peg-leg Cummings's spare leg and not one ripped from a corpse! It was quite a joke afterwards that Steyning had a man who had lost the same leg in action twice!"

"I must say that I don't remember any serious damage to the school. There was a bit. Some of the panes of glass were broken in the conservatory outside Room 8 and I think that some were broken elsewhere. The Library ceiling came down and fell on to the 6th Form class in Lower Library, to the later amusement of the ranks of juniors when word got round, but that is about all."

"Paul Brown says that he saw a beam in Big School jump clear of the wall, but settle back into place. That could have been nasty!"

"Just a bit!"

"I suppose that everyone went to the air raid shelters after the bomb dropped in case there were more to come, but I can't remember how long we were in there."

"John Sanford says that people were late for lunch because of this incarceration. His letter sounded a bit indignant on the subject. Spam fritters, or whatever, should in his view have taken precedence over mere bombs!"

"Hollins did get permission to go home at once to see that his mother was OK, but that was only a hundred yards from any of our shelters and I expect that he was told to go back to one as soon as he had checked."

"I do remember Geoffrey coming up and telling me to change into my Cubs uniform and go with him and others to search for valuables in the area around the damaged cottages. I actually found some keys, which was satisfying."

"It was pretty amazing that only two people were killed. There was Mrs Richardson who was sitting in her doorway, waiting for her husband to come home for lunch, and a Home Guard officer from Ashington who was smashed against a mounting block by the blast. There were a lot of very shaken folk and a few with some injuries, but just the two actually killed. Half-an-hour later and a lot would have been at home for lunch."

"A real regret of the boys was the loss of Mrs Eaton's sweet shop, which was on the school end of the cottages. She did put all the stock she salvaged into temporary premises in the High Street, but that was no good if you were coming from, or going to, the station."

"Fine. I think that we have got that all sorted into some reasonable state, but what of Riedel? What of he?"

"We can dismiss at once any thought that his face was recognised. That is an impossibility. I know that Geoffrey feels in his bones that it was one of the Riedels, but there is no proof because the surviving Luftwaffe records do not hold that kind of detail. From all that we have discussed so far, I am sure we can discount the theory that the raid was an abortive attack on the school and so disregard the threat to 'come back with a bomb', at least in the sense of attacking the school with it. However, let me do some 'supposing'. Let us suppose that one of the Riedels did join the Luftwaffe and that he flew FW 190s. If we now assume that a raid was planned to damage the RM Commandos in Chantry Green House, who better to undertake it than a young pilot who had spent two years at a school within a hundred yards or so of the target. Being a boarder, he was familiar with the detail of the countryside for a three mile radius of the school and, given a fixed point such as Chanctonbury Ring, could home in with ease. A further supposition must be that those who planned the raid knew of this connection, or that he heard about it and volunteered. There are a lot of 'ifs' in this, but stranger things have happened. The myth can take on a new lease of life, but with the silver lining that, although he came back with a bomb, he made damned sure that the school was not affected badly and had absolutely no thought at all of machine-gunning former playmates as they ran down the fire escape to the shelters."

"Do you know, Jean Scragg would have liked that idea. She was always quick to counter the thought that Riedel came back to bomb the school, with the hope that he was instead the pilot who flew over Steyning several times and then went out to sea to drop his bomb-load. Your 'supposing' would let me keep my intuition that it was Riedel and at the same time have let Jean keep her hope of his compassion. No proof, as you say, but it is a nice thought and a plausible one."

"I read somewhere that Lord Haw-Haw said in one of his broadcasts 'We have not forgotten Steyning'. Perhaps this was what he meant."

"The history books would barely support that! He was really rather poor at getting the detail right, I understand, and used generalities mixed with a few odd facts, such as noting that a certain town clock was five minutes slow, to cause uncertainty and anxiety, but you could be right. I believe that he used to live quite near to Steyning and, if so, was probably just firing a random shot into the air."

"There are just a couple of things mentioned in the written accounts which I have not told you. First, the vicar claimed that a Saxon stone by the chancel arch in the church had been moved by the blast. I am sorry to say that although the stone was moved, the motive force was two members of Holland House rather than Germanic explosives!"

"That does not surprise me at all! Was it what they call the Steyning Stone? You know, the one which is now in the church porch. It is pretty hefty. I remember that they found it when they were renewing the heating system for the church during the summer holidays in 1938, I think. It was around then anyway."

"I have a vague recollection of something much smaller which was kept in the church near the pulpit, so it was possibly that. Anyway, that is immaterial."

"The second point I had in mind is the whole business of post-traumatic shock. This was virtually discounted in those days, but I think that Sanford had it right when he says that they got over the shock by going to look at the damage and by talking about it amongst themselves."

"Do you know, for something like that particular incident, I think that the home-made therapy he describes did as much good as today's intensive counselling would have done; possibly more."

"Perhaps I'll raise it with Paddy Burges-Watson. He went on to specialise in battle trauma, didn't he? He should have some interesting thoughts on the subject. My motto is that if you find an Old Boy with specialist talents, you use them!"

"Right, that seems to be as far as we can go. We now need to sell it all to Chris Tod at the Museum! Thank you both for your time and effort."

CHAPTER 8

Friendly Fire

Apart from the Church Street bomb and the generally perceived threat of invasion, life in Steyning was not changed a great deal by the Germans. The activities of the British Army and its allies had more profound effects. Battle training areas closed off large tracts of the Downs and disrupted farming there. Buildings of all sorts were requisitioned for use by the forces including Wiston House and the surrounding park and Wappingthorn. The soldiers stationed in the area and those passing through, affected the day-to-day lives of local inhabitants. In Steyning, it was probably the Canadian troops who made the greatest impact. In 1941, Sussex was taken over by Canadians under Montgomery's overall command, to defend the area in the event of an invasion. They were unsung heroes and given scant attention by those reporting on military events. For example, the book produced by the Ministry of Information after the war which presents a selection of outstanding facts and figures, largely ignores the Canadian contribution in spite of the fact that Canada had mobilised 1.5 million into its armed forces out of a total population of 12 million; had given $4 billion in loans; and had produced more than 750,000 military vehicles. Canadians from the Steyning area were involved in the disastrous raid on Dieppe in August 1942 where so many lost their lives. Of the 6000 troops involved, 5000 were Canadians. Over 900 Canadians were killed; there were about 2000 taken prisoner and of the 2000 or so who returned, only 300 were unharmed. In Steyning, the Canadians are still remembered with some affection – and earlier affections led a number of young ladies from the town to be living now in Canada. It was not one-way traffic! So many Canadians stayed in Sussex after the war that it was said that, in the event of a third world war, Canada need not send troops over here but just their uniforms!

The boys at the Grammar School were affected too, but their priorities differed from those of most adults. The soldiers were a source of delicacies such as sweets. They also left in their wake a trail of unused or unexploded ordnance, more avidly sought by boys even than sweets. There was a brisk trade too in relics from crashed aircraft and in fragments of shrapnel. The battle training areas were out of bounds, of course, when in use and, of course, these bounds were broken regularly, sometimes with near fatal consequences. Demonstrations were sometimes laid on by the forces and enjoyed by all, especially by those lucky enough to become involved personally in rides in tanks or operating guns. The school's Cadet Force had its own crop of martial demonstrations and brought about a considerable desertion from the Scouts, to the annoyance of the Scoutmaster. Senior boys in the Cadets became involved also with the Home Guard. The fire-watchers liaised with the ARP. Waste paper was collected and funds raised for the war effort – although one boy records, unrepentantly, that he has not given a farthing to Steyning's Wings for Victory campaign because all his spare cash had been spent on chips. All of this was treated more as a bit of excitement and a change from the normal school routine than as anything else.

Everyone at the school during the war has his own anecdotes about some aspect of these activities. Listening to them one begins to believe firmly in guardian angels. Few boys were hurt and no-one from the school was killed by friendly fire or by home-made explosive devices however hard they appeared to try.

It takes very little to get Old Boys from those years to talk about their adventures with high explosives. It does take more effort to extract accounts of less dramatic events. However, at one informal gathering of locally-based Old Boys in a Worthing pub, a cluster of older participants was recalling the retreat of the BEF in 1940.

"Were you involved in manning the tea point which we set up at the bottom of Burdock's Slope for the soldiers retreating from Dunkirk?" asked one, "We couldn't give them much more than just tea, but we did our bit to show appreciation and cheer them up."

"I do remember the tea point, as you call it, but the soldiers were not from Dunkirk."

"Yes they were. I'm talking about 1940, you know!"

"Exactly! Now think back. What were the soldiers in and did they have guns?"

"In army trucks, mostly and there were guns and limbers being towed. I remember the guns and wanted a chance to look at one properly."

"My Lord, I rest my case! The main part of the BEF, nearly 350,000 men was indeed evacuated from Dunkirk in late May-early June. They were landed mainly at Dover and Folkestone and lost everything other than personal arms. Many had lost those too. Some days later, smaller groups of men, with their equipment, were taken off from St Valery, Le Harve and Cherbourg and most of them were landed at Newhaven and Shoreham. It was some of these who came up through Steyning."

"Well I never! I didn't know that. Were they large numbers who came off later?"

"No. Unfortunately, I think we are talking about 45,000 at maximum and they were brought back between June 10 and 18."

"Wherever they came from, I got into trouble with my Mum over them," said another, "I met a couple one morning who asked where they could find any food and told them to go to our house. Well, Mum gave them something and off they toddled, but spread the word that here was grub. My Mum was puzzled for the whole day why hungry soldiers kept appearing. I was stupid enough to tell her what I had done and there was a bit of a scene. She took it in good heart though – just!"

"Not all the Dunkirk lot went to Dover or Folkestone," chipped in a third, "Our house was in a state of worry for days because my brother was in the BEF and we knew that his unit was at Dunkirk and we had no news although we saw other members of his regiment around. Then we got a message from Liverpool that he was OK and up there. The ship which picked him up had gone there and I wouldn't be that surprised to hear that the skipper had done so to avoid having to go back!"

"Do you know, in some ways those were jolly exciting days. We had no real idea of the seriousness of the situation and it was all a bit of a game. I reckon that at some points the school held enough high explosive to flatten it. We picked stuff up all over the place."

"Stuart-Clark thought that the school had a lot of explosives in it too! Do you recall the police search of the place?"

"I do remember one, vividly. It was after a dire warning that anyone found with explosives would be expelled, so I think there would have been earlier purges which I can't bring back to mind. Anyway, we all had to go to stand by our lockers and I had a cannon shell in mine and was terrified of it being found and my being chucked out. By luck and dexterity I was able to open the locker while standing with my back to it and managed to smuggle the shell out before the searchers came."

"A cannon shell is about nine inches long! How did you manage?"

"Stuck it in my trousers pocket and hoped for the best."

"A case of 'Are you pleased to see me, or is that a cannon shell in your pocket?' eh!"

"No change from 1943! Still got a mind like a one way track to the sewage works!"

"Actually, I remember Dicky Wiseman saying that he had to do the 'backs to the locker and wiggle out incriminating evidence' trick too and probably in the same inspection. In his case it was a .303 round and a packet of Woodbines, which were easier to palm than a cannon shell."

"The same sort of thing happened to me. The search for some reason missed my tuck box which had quite a bit in it. I got scared and took the lot out in a plain wrapper, so to speak, and ditched it in the mill-pond on the way up to the rifle range. For all I know, it is still there."

"Did it include the famous PIAT? Have the rest of you heard that friend Rodney discovered this live anti-tank device on the edge of Amberley Wild Brooks near to Wiggonholt when pretending to be a Scout or something similar and slept with it under his pillow to prevent anyone stealing it from him?"

"You need to have grammar school brains to think of that! Imagine the phone conversation: 'Stuart-Clark from Steyning here Mrs Cox. I am sorry to have to tell you that your son seems to have lost his head'."

"The PIAT may well have been a part of that hoard."

"Sennitt got away with it by a fluke when they found some mortar bombs in his locker. Scragg asked him if there was any reason why he should not be expelled. In desperation he said that he had not heard the announcement. Scragg checked and found that he had indeed been off school with measles at the critical time. Sennitt had completely forgotten about that and, of course, knew the edict well from his friends. A very lucky escape!"

"I remember finding a small finned thing on the Downs near to Shoreham and took it home to Henfield on the train. When I dismantled it, I found it was a magnesium flare with a small parachute attached. The magnesium burned well! We used the parachute in the playground with a weight attached to the strings, chucking it into the air and watching it come down. Then it went on to the HM's lawn and was captured."

"Are you sure? As I recall, it got caught up on the electricity cable between the main school and the gym and hung there for ever."

"You could be right, but I thought it was the lawn which meant that it was lost to us."

"No. What happened was that it was retrieved from the lawn without permission and to avoid it drifting over there again we took it to the top of Burdock's Slope and with the very first throw it got caught on the electricity cable and, as you said, hung there for ever."

"We used to collect failed signal flares, gut them and crush up the bit inside. You could make a good display using them on a Bunsen burner."

"Another regular game was sticking live rounds of .303 or .22 ammo into holes in the wood of the bike shed, or between a couple of stones and then trying to set them off by hitting them with a nail mounted in a long piece of wood. The cartridge case would go high into the air."

"Richard Tomkies came to grief like that. In fact he was lucky not to have been killed. The Canadians had 'liberated' a case of .22 ammunition for his father to use to shoot for the pot and he would take a handful and prat around with them, setting them off. Well, a piece of cartridge case pierced his eye and skidded around inside, where, he says, it remains to this day."

"The same could have happened to me! We would find butterfly bombs which had not gone off, loop some string round them and pull from a distance. One which didn't go off, we took back to school and stored under the floorboards of the dormitory."

"I wonder if it is still there."

"Interesting thought!"

"Were you involved in the parachute flare incident? We had found this mortar round which held a flare which, when shot into the air, was supposed to come down slowly on its parachute, so illuminating the general scene for a long time. Well, as usual, we gutted it to see what was inside and made good use of the flare and the parachute. We then decided to let the propelling charge off by the bike shed, using the board and nail technique. The actual size of the charge was wildly underestimated. There was a huge bang and we all ran like rabbits before a Master or prefect could arrive. When we went back, we found bits of the casing embedded in almost everything nearby. I can't explain why none of us had chunks in us, but it certainly made us a little bit wiser."

"Wuzzo Wisden told me that he would collect stuff from the battle training area, take the innards out and construct his own explosive devices with them. He said that someone else doing this blew the door off the chemi lab fume cupboard and that Buff Bennett was not very happy about it!"

"I think he was talking about Zwartouw, who was experimenting making some liquid explosive. When he lifted it up, it exploded, splashing into his eyes. Buff grabbed him and stuck his face under a tap, which may have saved his sight."

"Good old Buff! I wonder what that liquid was."

"All that I can think of which goes pop if you tap it or disturb it in any way is nitrogen tri-chloride. The only thing is that it is one of the most powerful chemical explosives known and a flask of that would have put half the school into orbit."

"That knowledge would have spurred Zwartouw on rather than deter him!"

"Does anyone else remember when an army lorry carrying shells caught fire on the A24 just outside Washington? It was a quarter of a mile from our house and the explosions went on for over half-an-hour. We took shelter in the house. A big chunk of shell landed right by the door and the garden had quite a lot of fragments scattered over it. No-one was hurt or killed though. That was bangs on a majestic scale, but I must admit a bit too close for me to enjoy properly, especially as Mother was nervous about it."

"I got a bit too close to the action once, myself. I was walking along, minding my business, when a mortar bomb went off a few yards to my left. It was soon followed by one going off to my right. I had strayed on to a range without noticing, but left it more rapidly than I had come! That was a problem with the battle training area and ranges; they were not fenced off. There were plenty of notices and there were flag poles which had red flags hoisted on them when the area was in use, but you could walk past without noticing if you were not paying attention."

"Reminds me of Bob Miller who got caught in front of a creeping barrage when he was looking for goodies on the battle training area. He had to run almost into Lancing to get away from it!"

"A group of us boarders was nearly taken out by live firing too. We were on the Bostal Road near to Maudlin Barn, which was inside the battle training area, when some smoke grenades arrived round it. We thought 'Great! Let's use the smoke screen to play at being soldiers attacking the barn.' So we went into our attack mode. We had just arrived, as it were, when all hell was let loose with bullets and mortar bombs whizzing around the place. Luckily there were some slit trenches dug there, perhaps earlier in the war by the Home Guards who had a station up there. We popped into them and it was some time before the army realised that it had an important section of Holland House pinned down and under fire. I draw a veil over the language, military, NCOs for the use of, which was then directed at us and the language pedagogical, Housemasters and Headmasters for the use of, to which we were subjected on our return to base. We were lucky both to survive as SGS pupils and to survive at all."

"I do get annoyed when I find the Ordnance Survey using names which none of us ever used for places. Maudlin Barn is down as New Hill Barn on the map I've got."

"I know what you mean and if you look closely it is in the 'wrong' place. The army battered it down, but it was rebuilt further from the road after the war and renamed. Before the war the OS had it as Hill Barn. We always called it Maudlin Barn because it belonged to Maudlin Farm."

"It is a pity that the original barn was destroyed. I gather that it had a mediaeval threshing floor in it."

"Is that so? That would not have deterred the Canadians! I heard a story that when one of them flattened a 500-year-old cottage with his tank when driving through a village, he expressed relief that it was only an old house which had been destroyed and not a new one!"

"Most of the troops I remember were Canadians. I loved them because they would give us sweets and the plane-spotting series from their Sweet Caporal cigarette packets."

"That's right and they would lay on parties for local kids up at Wiston House – candies, cakes, hat badges, all sorts. We were given a baseball bat on one occasion. They taught us to play baseball on the Playing Field and that was great."

"I think that their Sussex HQ was at Windlesham House School just off the A24 between Findon and Washington and that here they specialised in petroleum warfare."

"That could explain the Bostal Road fire trap for tanks!"

"You could well be right. Their specialists certainly helped to construct ammo dumps and underground bases for the Special Units and the Home Guard and probably helped with things like unarmed combat training and knife work."

"I don't know about that, but we would play football with them and you had to watch out for their army boots!"

"They would give us rounds of .303 ammo and, as someone mentioned just now, if you were on the right side of them, they were not above 'liberating' ammunition for people to use to shoot rabbits and pigeons."

"I am not sure if it was them or some of our soldiers who were bivouacked in St Cuthman's Field and for some reason sorted through their packs and discarded a whole lot of magnets. There was a bag-full which one of the boys was given. Next day they were for sale in the school at 3d a pair, but the price went up as the stocks went down. I still have and use the pair I got for 3d!"

"You knew it when they hit the town! I saw the train guard at Steyning station lock groups of drunken Canadians into their compartments for their own safety when they were off to sample the doubtful pleasures of Brighton. But they were usually just kind and friendly. There was a good deal of singing in the Norfolk Arms though!"

"One Canadian soldier wrote after the war, that the publicans of

Fletching, Piltdown and the Kings Head deserved medals and wound stripes. I don't think it got quite that riotous in Steyning."

"There was a story – and I'm not sure whether it is true or not – that a group of them from Wiston saw half-a-dozen prams outside Grigg's grocery store and swapped the babies round for a lark. They were disciplined, but no-one is entirely sure whether all the babies were reared by the right parents."

"Come on! Pull the other one!"

"Well, that's what I heard."

"They were all right. I used to help the local carrier collect and deliver their laundry and on one very cold day a soldier took off his khaki gloves and gave them to me. I wore them with enormous pride and to the jealousy of my mates for months afterwards. Odd how a little kindness like that sticks in your mind."

"One let me have a go at driving a road roller with which he was flattening out beach shingle on the track leading from Mouse Lane by Charlton Court Farm up on to the Downs. He had asked me to get him a light for his fag from one of the cottages since they were getting fed up with him going to ask. They made other shingle roads in the battle training areas too and you can still find traces of the beach pebbles up there."

"They had regular film shows in St Andrew's Hall in Jarvis Lane and let us go in to watch. I really enjoyed that because there were not many other film shows in Steyning. A film was quite a novelty. These days TV has made everyone a bit bored by films, but it wasn't like that then."

"Just before D-Day they laid on a bit of a party in St Andrew's Hall. I got given a lot of chewing gum."

"Did Sennitt ever tell you about his adventure with chewing gum? No? Well, he had been greatly impressed by the gum given to him by the Canadians who were chasing his sister. His father then took him with him to his chemist's shop in Ealing and he had a good time wandering round inside the shop with its flagons of coloured water and so on. He noticed some packets of gum and pocketed them. He thinks in retrospect that his father knew, but kept his mouth shut. He says that the gum was quite good, but he began to understand the meaning of the word 'laxative' early next morning!"

"I'm glad that he pigged the lot himself and didn't bring it to school to share with his pals!"

"It wasn't all Canadians though. Our own lot were always about the place, especially in the build-up to D-Day. They were not as generous as the Canadians, but afforded us a few good spectacles. I'll never forget the school shaking as a column of tanks went up Church Street from the railway station. They were brought there by train and were off, I would guess, to the battle training area behind the Round Hill."

"I remember being rather amused when a tank failed to judge the corner properly by Mouse Lane and embedded itself in the bakery, but I don't expect that the owners of the bakery thought it very funny."

"It was awful, wasn't it, when they shelled the town by accident from the tank range. No-one knew just what was happening at first. We were in church at the time and a shell landed nearby and killed a boy – not one of ours – in a garden just west of the church. We were all run back to school in a crocodile of sorts and told to go into the shelters. Our relief at missing the sermon was tempered by hunger and frustration because we were kept there until this friendly fire ceased instead of enjoying our Sunday lunch."

"That took quite a while! I gather from the Press reports that when the first shells arrived, the police were told that mortar bombs were landing in Steyning. When this was relayed to the army, the officer in charge of the tank range took no notice because they were not using mortars and so thought it nothing to do with him. He did get the tanks to shorten their range as a precaution, but carried on firing. This meant that instead of landing by the church the next strays landed near the police station in the cricket field and allotments. By this time it had been realised that it was 75mm shells which were landing and not mortar bombs. Further representations were made and the firing stopped."

"It wasn't just the boy, Arthur ('Brubber') Chandler, who was killed. Another shell landed amongst a group of about 40 Home Guards who were doing gas training near the rifle range. One of them was killed and others injured."

"Two people killed. That was the same number as were killed by the Church Street bomb!"

"It could have been a lot worse. Thirteen shells landed in or near to the town and five failed to explode, including one which landed in the gas works."

"Ah, that may explain something which was bothering me. I recall that a range instructor had to observe all bursts. If so many were overshooting, these missing bursts should have been obvious. However, if nearly half of the shots on target failed to explode, as did nearly half of the ones landing in Steyning, over-shooting would not be so evident. Did this come out in the inquiry?"

"I can't say. In the only reports I have seen, the army clammed up because a military inquiry was about to take place and I have seen no account of its findings."

"There was another oddity about this incident. I remember Waine saying how surprised his parents had been to read about it in the Monday papers and I think that it was on the radio news the night before. The authorities ordered this to be done to nip in the bud any rumours that an invasion had begun! Normally things like this were hushed up."

"Quite early on I recall a demonstration with a few tanks brought along and you could ride in them and, if you could drive a tractor you could have a go at a tank. It was up on the Downs."

"Yes, I was there and banged my head on the roof of the turret when we went over a bump!"

"Sandy Bridges says that it was the ride in a Valentine at this demo which led to him joining the Royal Armoured Corps. He was commissioned out of Sandhurst towards the end of the war and served as a troop commander in Northern Italy, so something came out of the event."

"I don't remember that, but there was another in Wiston Park where the Pioneers showed us how to get a tank out of a deep ditch and how to use walkie-talkies. That was good fun."

"I remember another time when they gave a demonstration of a 25-pounder gun up on the Playing Field and fired a few blanks. I was able to play around with it. Not loaded, of course."

"Thank God for small mercies!"

"There were lots of demonstrations and hands-on events put on for the Cadets. We fired mortars and flame-throwers; did small arms shooting at a range in Bramber; and went canoeing on the clay pits at Small Dole with the Commandos. That was really good. Most of the senior boys wanted to join in and there was a mass defection from the Scouts which didn't please SBS at all!"

"It wasn't just the seniors who wanted to join. I did, mainly so that I could have a go at playing a drum, but was only old enough to join the Cubs!"

"Everybody say 'Ahhh!'"

"There were all sorts of field exercises too. You could use blanks in the rifles and throw thunder-flashes. We got up to the rifle range too and I must say it was a bit scary working the targets with bullets slamming in a few feet above you."

"I do remember that someone let two thunder-flashes off in the garden of No. 7. Authority took a dim view, but I don't think anyone was found guilty and punished."

"I don't know who did it, even now. I expect that the usual Dire Warning was given and the matter dropped."

"Someone demolished a phone box with explosives too, but I'm sure that wasn't any of the Cadets: more likely to be the soldiers. I don't think that the Home Guard would have done it."

"We used to go to a house in Dog Lane which had a long cellar set up as a .22 rifle range. I am pretty sure it was a Home Guard place although the ARP used it too. They were always around there at night."

"It was on one night exercise that we saw some strange strings of lights in the sky. We found out later that these were the first doodle-bugs on their way to London."

"There was an annual Cadets' camp where we joined up with others. That was a bit more spit and polish and people like our Cadet Sergeant Major, Leo Cruttenden, came into their own. He had a voice like one of the Bulls of Bashan!"

"About a year after it was started our Cadets joined up with Shoreham Grammar School and three of the coastal town units to form the 6th Cadet Battalion of the Royal Sussex Regiment. This vastly complicated all administrative arrangements and the total chaos of the Battalion Camp in 1945 illustrates the point!"

"I think that some of that had been sorted out by 1946 when we went to a huge Camp near Ruabon where Cadets from all over were there."

"I used to play the bugle! In spite of that I rose to the giddy heights of Corporal."

"Old Bowman was probably tone deaf!"

"Yes, of course it was the Bow who started the Cadets going! It was at the start of the summer term in 1943. I remember the notice going up on the board and that it said that the Officer Commanding was 2/Lt FE Bowman and the Second in Command was 2/Lt HB Collison. He and Collison kept it running well, but after the Bow left, Collison took over with Idris David as his number two. It soon fell apart and was disbanded in 1947/48. It was odd really, because the Bow looked anything but a military man, but he did a good job with the Cadets."

"He was in charge of the little rifle range we set up in the air raid shelter by the Woodwork Shop. I used to help him sift the bullets out of the sand and melt the lead out of them to sell."

"All the firearms and ammo was kept in the cellar under the gym changing room. It was called the Armoury. Then the Scouts kept some of their gear in it when the Cadets were disbanded, but it was still called the Armoury into the early 1950s. Then, much later on, it was used as a tuck shop run by the boys, but that was then relocated in part of the old kitchens when the new Dining Hall was built."

"Were the bugles and drums kept there too? I have a vague feeling that they were stored in one of the air raid shelters."

"Do you know, I can't remember. I would have thought that it would have been a bit damp in the shelters for drums – and would have tempted fate since the boys would have had easy access to them. I would guess they went into the Armoury, or into Bowman's rooms."

"I found that there were advantages to having been in the Cadets when it came to National Service. I had got my marksman's credentials and was a corporal in the Cadets. After seven days in the army, I was made up to an acting, unpaid lance-corporal. I might say too that National Service was a doddle after several years of coping with the hazards of life as a Steyning boarder!"

"Just let me butt in with an aside," I said, "There was no Cadet Force in the school from the late 1940s all the way through the 1950s and 60s and into the Comprehensive School era after that. However, there is a Cadet Force in the present school."

"Good for them. I hope that, in spite of all the nonsense about health and safety these days, they get as much fun and adventure out of it as we did!"

CHAPTER 9

War? What War?

The general impression which one gets from reading memoirs, or through talking to those at the school during the war, is that the school maintained a perfectly ordinary scholastic existence and was sheltered from outside affairs by its insularity. The teaching staff tried to act as normal schoolmasters in spite of their extra-curricular war-time activities. The domestic staff kept the usual time-table of meals going and the buildings in good repair and as clean as the boys allowed. Rationing did make for difficulties; there were sporadic attacks from the air; the boys did get hold of a lot of ordnance and enjoyed the exotic thrill of the company of serving soldiers. These were simply add-on extras to normal school life. When it came to the news of the war itself with, in the early days, the feeling of threat; the constant losses; the erosion of Empire; the changes in social structure; the danger to parents, siblings and friends from air raids and from active service; all were somehow distant as if they were being viewed through the wrong end of a telescope. The long term, so far as the boys were concerned, was the summer term!

Regardless of what was going on outside, boys attended to class-work with varying degrees of diligence and ragged the masters when the opportunities presented themselves. The latter was perhaps on a bit more of a generous scale than before or after the war because a lot of the teachers were stop-gap ones and had wider chinks in their armour than those in the school before hostilities began, or in those returning to, or joining the staff afterwards.

Although travel was restricted, trips out of school were still made. Ways were found of getting round the 'no camping within 10 miles of the coast' regulation by letting the Scouts have a breather away from the school by using barns at Wiggonholt where water fights between two neighbouring yards were enjoyed until the Scoutmaster stepped in to avoid total flooding. In something of a revolt against the emphasis on sporting prowess, the less athletic boys set up a Rambling Club in 1939/40 and went out into the locality to examine archaeological sites and undertake field work; to do brass-rubbing; to help with Stanley

Bayliss Smith's ornithological work and so on. In 1944 a Debating Society was begun and resolved to the satisfaction of the boys such thorny questions as to whether jazz or classical music were best (jazz); whether it was the Arts or the Sciences which brought the greater benefits (Sciences); whether all Germans were to blame for the war and should be punished (yes – unforgiving and media-led young savages!); and whether a prefectorial system was good and necessary in a school (yes – possibly because prefects would have led the discussion!).The exceptionally cold winters of 1939/40 and 1946/7, although adding to the difficulties and discomforts, gave also opportunities for adventurous play seized on by boys, staff and local inhabitants alike. Lack of traffic on the roads gave boys the opportunity to cycle with greater freedom and farming and forestry camps in Warwickshire and Shropshire were reached on bicycles by some of the boys.

Just before the beginning of the war, the House system was changed with the four existing Houses slimmed down to three with the loss of Cissa and all the boarders being assigned to Holland. The day boys were split between Chancton and Cuthman. Over-crowding of the boarders was alleviated by Coombe Court falling vacant in 1939 and being taken over as supplementary accommodation under the supervision of Mr Bennett who moved in with his mother. In 1940, the school took over No. 7 Church Street, which gave a little more space for boarders and a staff flat. The school continued to grow throughout the war years and numbers rose from 169 boys in July 1939 to 258 in July 1945, of whom 76 were boarders, twenty more than in 1939.

Owing to wartime restrictions, the Library was in constant difficulties to find and purchase any new books. A similar lack in supplies of games kit led to the Old Boys being asked to search out any unwanted football boots and shirts and donate them to a common pool. However, in this atmosphere of austerity, exhibitions of local contemporary art were put on in the school and proved so successful that they entered the school calendar as regular features through the 1940s-1960s.

Overall there was a surprising degree of normality in school life and that is a tribute to the staff and to the boys themselves. Fred Franklin sums it up in his recollections by saying that at school they were sheltered from reality in their little cocoon. Only on leaving and getting involved in war work, or when news came of friends killed, did it strike home that outside the school things were **not** normal.

Another day and another informal gathering in a Lancing pub. It is noticeable that the more Old Boys meet up with one another the more day-to-day are the subjects discussed, although usually we get back to schooldays in the end. Health was on the agenda this time and more of that later. I arrived more or less at the same time as a newcomer to these meetings whose glasses had steamed up. As he took them off he glanced round and with glad cries made his way across. "My God, James! You look just the same." Then, putting his glasses back on and looking again, "Oh no you don't!"

"I don't think that any of us can lay much claim to have kept in the same physical condition since we left. I huff and puff walking up hills I used to run up at school. Still, some have weathered better than others."

In a corner a small group of the older generation was chewing the fat about the war.

"Do you know something? In retrospect life was amazingly normal at school during the war. They chucked in some innovations too which appealed, like giving us the last period off once a week for Form Games on the Field. It was the only time apart from the School matches that boarders and day boys played on the same sides and skipping Latin officially for a game of football was very popular! Yes, there were things we got involved in which only the war threw up, but the routine just kept going regardless. I'm glad that it did, because routine and set rules are very reassuring. Start mucking them about and no-one knows where the accepted boundaries are to behaviour or what the next day may bring, which is worry-making. We knew that lunch would be at 1.00; that we had Charlie for History first period on Monday (Hurray! A good rag in prospect!) and Scraggy for English second period (Oh my God, I hope I have done my prep!); and that school would finish at twenty to four. We just got on with normal life which helped protect us from the war."

"We were aware of the war all right, but it didn't seem part of our lives really. I recall that when there was news in 1944 that the Second Front had started, Peter Bloomfield asked 'What's the Second Front?'"

"We did get involved with war work sometimes. Were you ever a member of the Toy Club?"

"I don't remember that one. What did it do?"

"Schools which had woodwork shops were asked to make toys for children who had lost everything in the blitz. Stuart-Clark was all for it and many boys joined in and we made a good range of toys which were sent off at the end of term. We even got 'thank you' letters from some of the families. It gave you a good feeling to think that you had brought pleasure to someone who had lost the lot."

"Steyning was very sheltered from the action too, which helped to separate us from things. Boyd-Livingston used to say it was an oasis of quiet compared with his home area in Kent, as do Cox about his home in Ealing and even Wiseman about Littlehampton."

"We did our best to liven things up. Do you remember when Mr Bowman was bending over in Big School to look at a boy's work, the one sitting behind, who had not seen him come in and thought he was another boy, stuck the point of his compass into his bum? He soon discovered his mistake!"

"Titch Mason – before he was Head Boy – had a trick of dropping fizzy lemonade tablets into inkwells to make them froth up over the victim's desk."

"He got away with it, I expect, but I was beaten for putting carbide into someone's inkwell in Latin and was banned from Latin thereafter. A positive to balance the negative of being caned!"

"I'll bet that it was Larynx Harris's class. Something must have snapped that time. He probably thought that you would light the acetylene and blow the class up."

"You have forgotten how scarce matches were. We even used to light the Bunsen burners in chemistry by dropping a pellet of potassium into water to give a flame."

"I heard from John Eveleigh not long ago, that one of his first inventions was a potassium-powered torpedo which had its trial run in the Bow's pond in No. 7 garden without killing any fish. John has 48 world-wide patents to his name now and probably regrets not having registered this at the time too."

"Do you remember how Mr Moore used to keep one or two lessons ahead in Maths which he had to take as well as PT and how some of the brighter sparks would read up lessons three or four ahead and ask awkward questions. Quite often he would struggle away with problems in the lesson and finally give up and go to the answers. You had to be a bit careful if you had him in the afternoon because he would have tanked up in the Three Tuns at lunch and could be a bit fiery. One of his nicknames was 'Three Tuns Moore'!"

"Major Child was another who kept just ahead of the field – or rather, he had virtually given up. It was boiling water for periods on end, or titrations. Sometimes he would demonstrate the pressure built up by steam by putting a syrup tin with a bit of water in it on a tripod over a Bunsen burner and banging the lid down. He seemed quite oblivious of the cowering ranks in the first couple of rows in the class! There was always that vague, benign smile on his face and 'Abominable boy!' on his lips."

"He had that trick with the special narrow-lined paper he dished out in class. Paper was very scarce, of course, but he seemed to have cornered his own supply. He would take a small stack out of the packet, lay it on the bench and rub his knuckle round in a circle near the middle of the sheets. After about five minutes had been wasted from the period, he would have made a splendid fan of the paper, which he would then find easy to separate into single sheets to give out."

"Yes, I do remember him doing that. One time he came in with a fresh ream of paper which he put on his desk and then left the room for some reason. When he came back, the whole lot had been snatched by the class. He then said 'I shall go out and come back in five minutes – and the paper will be back when I return'. In fact, some 80% was returned, but some of the bolder spirits had a nice little bonus of paper."

"We got a bit of a bonus of a different kind over Divinity when Harry-Parry taught us. He wasn't a member of staff properly but just a visiting chaplain. A cartoon vicar in a way, but very pleasant. He got us reading Dorothy Sayers' *Man born to be King* with boys taking the parts. Much better than the usual Divinity lessons, although I do remember one, I think with Stuart-Clark, when we had a talk about polygamy followed by a lecture on faith and behaviour, all clearly with the town girls in mind. That kept us awake at least. It was the nearest I ever got to sex education at school and makes up about the least useful bits of my knowledge of the topic!"

"We got up to plenty outside the classroom. Dim Smith reminded me of the time SBS whacked him, Wallis and Courtney-Bennett for winding bog paper round the playground by heaving it out from the rolls in the cubicles, while singing 'Yo-ho heave ho…'. He had just got back to the cubicle, still towing the paper, when he realised that the only one singing was him and was confronted by an indignant SBS. He got the whack too when SBS caught him making apple-pie beds for the inhabitants of Long Dorm just before the boarders' Christmas Feast. He then had to sit next to SBS in the feast – or try to sit, at least."

"That trinity were at the bottom of the pile very often when there was mischief in the air, but there were others – McCarthy, for instance. He got beaten by the HM for ragging Moore in prep and decided to skip ragging Charlie Chaplin next evening when Charlie was on duty. The following day, his diary records 'Sat next to Pocock and Bow-ragged'. Good resolution lasted just one day!"

"There was also Andrew Jary, God help us! Where the rest of us in Form 3 were the bane of dear old Charlie's life, Jary was a sort of Form 3 all on his own. Utterly incorrigible, uncontrollable - a Borstalian if ever there was one. But well liked by us."

"It wasn't just the masters you could have fun with. I was in the prefects' room once when Mr Savage came in to stoke the boiler and to pass the time of day asked him, pointing to the thermometer on top, whether it was centigrade or Fahrenheit. 'Nah, it's anthracite, mate, it runs on anthracite.'"

"Do you know," I cut in, "I have heard that same story, given in the first person, with as many different locations as there are boilers in the school and placed in a variety of years from the 1940s right through the 1950s. Either this entered the school's mythology, or Savage was having a regular and secret little joke on us!"

"I must say that in that dreadful winter of 1946/47 the school was like the Arctic because of lack of fuel. Coombe Court was a nightmare, but the rest of the place was icy too."

"It gave us some smashing tobogganing though in the Three-cornered Field on the Round Hill. If you had a good toboggan you had to watch out for the concrete trough by the bottom gate. One boy broke his arm on it and we had to pad it with old mattresses after that."

"Were you there when Willie Goble had a go on Den Carter's very fast toboggan? He sat straight up on it, not lying on his stomach like the rest of us, with his hat on and an umbrella in his hand, and shot off down the course. He looked something like a latter-day knight setting off to slay dragons or to joust!"

"We had good fun, but not over such a long period, in the cold winter of 1939/40 when half the town went skating on Wiston Pond for a couple of weeks at least. Then, just after the thaw had set in, there was snow and the toboggans came out in force and Scraggy appeared on skis! Someone got from the Three-cornered Field right down Newham Lane, into the High Street and ended up by Dog Lane. It was the longest run I heard about, but it was on a special toboggan with metal runners. Must be a good mile."

"Tobogganing could get you into trouble. One of the really serious crimes I was beaten for was for giving a girl from Worthing High School a go on my toboggan! This rated an even higher tariff than collecting a ball from the Headmaster's Lawn without permission!"

"Talking of punishments, while most masters would get you to write lines or do 'sides' for looking out of the window at aeroplanes, SBS would ask what kind of a plane it was and then say 'A Blenheim was it? Then draw me 100 Blenheims by break tomorrow'."

"If you got sent out of the class for any reason, you hoped that after the statutory 5-10 minutes you would be called back in and given lines before the HM found you on one of his prowls. If he did, it was three of the best! If your class-work was bad, you could be put on Daily Report."

"I had forgotten about Daily Report until you mentioned it! You were given this blue notebook, weren't you, and after every period the master had to give you a mark from *Vic Satis* to *Non Satis*. The HM examined the book weekly to decide whether encouragement of a more direct kind was called for. I was only put on Report once, but it was a nerve-wracking chore."

"I reckon that the staff did all that they could to keep things as normal as possible for us and also made sure that the boarders in particular got to do interesting things. Freda Sage, for example, occasionally took boys to the Theatre Royal in Brighton. The plays were great, but a real attraction was the interval with cups of tea and Nice biscuits."

"They tried 'tea dances' with Worthing High School for Girls for a bit. Trouble was that we were all rather shy and sat around while all the staff danced. They called it 'chaperoning'. I saw that Freda was quite in demand and we noted the masters who danced with her."

"Did any of you hear about her and Johnny in the early 1950s?" I asked, "No? Well, they both attended some grand educational event down in Brighton and the local paper reported on it. Amongst the tedious listing of who was there, the article said, 'Also present was the Headmaster of Steyning Grammar School, Mr John Scragg, with one of his mistresses.' The staff collected a lot of copies and kept posting them on the notice-board every time that Johnny took one down."

"Good show! A lot had fantasies about Freda!"

"We had some wild idea about her being a German spy and tried to get compromising comments from her. I also remember the theory that Masters were involved in smuggling and the black market and that loot was stashed round the school. We lifted up floorboards in the dormitories in the search for the hiding places. At least our imaginations were active!"

"Didn't Freda gain fame during an impromptu bathing session?" I asked, "I seem to remember that Rodney told me about it. That's right isn't it Rodney?"

"Indeed it is! We were on a Junior Walk and went up Mouse Lane to Wiston Springs, you know, the pond in a little spinney to the left as you go into the Park – not the main Pond. It was a hot day; the water was deep, clean and inviting and we were allowed to strip off and go in. Then one boy got cramp and was in a bit of trouble, so Freda stripped down to her panties and bra to be prepared to go in and pull him out. Unfortunately, he recovered and got himself out before she could dive in. I fell off the log I was riding on with shock! Chris Passmore says that SBS was with us and he did strip off completely and heaved the boy out, but I don't remember that he was with us. However we all had our eyes sticking out like organ stops looking at Freda and the King himself could have been cavorting around naked without our noticing!"

"One of the problems during and just after the war was that we could not go sea-bathing because of all the coastal defences. We did go occasionally as a treat to the King Alfred Baths in Hove."

"There were also unauthorised swimming parties in the clay pits by Small Dole. You know, the places where the frogmen trained. It wouldn't be allowed now and was frowned on then, but we didn't care if the weather was hot!"

"Looking back on what we did, I surprised that we didn't pick up some pretty nasty infections. I used to swim in the Adur and never even thought about the town's sewage works which put barely treated stuff into the river upstream."

"We used to get all sorts of odd infections at school. Most were flu types of virus, I think, but in early 1939 half the school was put out of action by them for what seemed like a couple of months. Then Bumps Bristow got scarlet fever and infected a fair number of boarders. Rodney Cox will know all about that because he was one of the victims. They were all confined to Room 8 as a kind of isolation ward."

"That's right! There were six of us whose swabs showed positive, myself, McCarthy, Paul Brown and three others and we had to wait ten days to see if anyone developed the disease. If they did, they were whisked off to hospital and the rest had to start the ten days again. We were only allowed out under supervision when everyone else was in class and when we went out for walks like that, the townsfolk were warned to keep clear! All in all we had to start our ten days three times and it meant our staying at the school for three or four days after the rest had gone home on holiday. I expect that the staff who had to stay to look after us were as disgruntled as we were! Eventually, we were disinfected thoroughly and sent home."

"Talking about illnesses, you look a bit under the weather, Dennis", I said, "I hope that there is nothing the matter."

"I am very pleased to report that what we had feared is not the matter. I had a colonoscopy this morning and it was all clear, but it was a bit shattering."

"You don't have to tell me! I can name your problem at once. It is called 'CleanPrep'!"

"I can see you have experienced it yourself. I hope that all was OK."

"Well, no it wasn't, but they had me in, unzipped me; slashed about with machetes in the jungle; stapled me together again; and have been pouring chemistry into me at intervals ever since. I am glad to say that although my colon is now a semicolon, I have yet to reach a full stop! One of the side effects of my treatment means that I now have no fingerprints! Which crime of the century do you recommend?"

"What about a local bank for starters? You could buy us all a round then!"

"The banks have lost all the money, so I don't think that is a profitable idea!"

"Be that as it may,but to return to CleanPrep, the best description of its effects that I know is that written by Dave Barry, an American writer. Over there it is called MoviPrep. He remarks that it must never fall into the hands of America's enemies and goes on to say that it is a laxative of nuclear proportions. You sip away at a litre of a liquid which tastes like a mixture of goat's spit and urinal cleanser with a hint of lemon and then take up residence in the toilet, still sipping. The instructions on the packet are, he says, written by someone with a strong sense of humour. They claim that after you drink it 'a loose, watery bowel movement may result'. This is like saying if you jump off your roof, you may experience contact with the ground. He goes on to ask if you have ever seen the space shuttle being launched. In the MoviPrep experience, you are the shuttle and after a bit you wish that the toilet had been fitted with seat-belts. There is more inside you than you thought was possible. You then have to sip another litre of the stuff and at this point your bowels journey into the future as you begin to eliminate food which you have not even eaten yet. All this is the evening before and you are allowed nothing other than clear liquids until your examination. You understand why Dennis is looking fragile!"

"I should say so. He obviously needs building up again. By the way, I was never accused of clean prep at school. Tom Pretheroe wrote alongside a page of my geometry prep which involved drawings of circles, tangents, radii and so on, 'I see that the birds' nesting season has started early this year.' Sarcastic blighter!"

"Did I hear a medical discussion?" chipped in another.

"Yes, Dennis had a colonoscopy this morning which gave him the all clear, but has left him shattered."

"Glad you are OK Dennis. I have never had one of those, but twice a year I get a gloved, medical digit shoved up me and wiggled about. Enough to make me glad that I am not gay. I can't imagine what a few feet of optic tubing with a camera and surgical instruments attached would be like and have no desire to find out."

"I'll bet that at least 90% of the company here today have experienced CleanPrep and/or the questing medical digit."

"At school, the equivalent was Matron's dose of castor oil with a splodge of sulphur added for good measure. That was the panacea, so far as I remember in the 1930s!"

"Impetigo is one thing I had and forgot to tell my mother. She turned up for sports day, or something, and nearly died of fright because my whole face was purple from the gentian violet used to treat it. Matron used to spend ages picking bits off me with tweezers. I didn't mind because I skipped a lot of prep."

"The thing was to get into sick bay for a bit if you had not done your prep or if detention loomed. There was a sure-fire way of getting a temperature so that Matron would scoop you up and shove you in for a day or two. You made good wads of blotting paper and put them into your socks under your insteps. If you walked about like that for a few hours, you were guaranteed a temperature to go with your mythical headache or whatever."

"Come on! I never heard of that when I was there. It sounds more like witchcraft than anything else to me!"

"I can assure you that it worked. How and why I have no idea."

"Well, we have come a long way in a short time. An Old Boy and a doctor, Nathaniel Blaker, writing around the turn of the 19th century was celebrating the fact that anaesthetics were now used in amputations and no longer did you get the patient to drink a bottle of rum and then be held down by six strong men. You could take your time whereas in the old days speed was of the essence, and far fewer people died, when he was writing, from post-operative shock or post-operative infection. Thank your lucky stars that you were not at school in the 1840s!"

Across the room, discussion still centred firmly on the 1940s.

"I think it was before your time, but the whole school had a day out walking on the Downs on Whit Monday in 1940. That was before the army took over half the Downs. The Government had decided that it would not be a Bank Holiday that year, but the school timetable had left the day blank. Stuart-Clark got together with John Scragg and they devised a route taking in the archaeological sites around Chanctonbury Ring, Park Brow and Cissbury. The day boys carried their own food and drink with them and SBS and 'Free Meals' Thompson used their cars to ferry the boarders' supplies from the school to Cissbury. The day boys on the whole rather pitied the boarders' fare, but were reluctant to part with their own goodies either as gifts or in exchange. Can't think why! It was a good day out and we learnt quite a bit about local history too."

"I think it was that walk which first got me interested in archaeology and I still like to walk up to Cissbury from time to time to try to recapture the mood of that day. Then, quite recently, I came across a poem which helped to do so. I can't quote it all from memory, but it is quite short and ends *'Two thousand years: time's slow explosion still scattering daggers and axeheads and dust of bones. / Quiet sounds: a drowsy burden of grasshoppers; the wind's thin bugle bending ranks of grass. / No shouting at the gate now: warriors silent, their long bronze trumpets choked with earth.'"*

"Yes, I like that. Who wrote it? Do you know?"

"There is a strong Steyning connection! Paul Coltman, the poet, taught English at the school from 1950 right through into the Comprehensive era. I think him under-rated as a poet myself. But going back to what we were talking about, it was not so free and easy from then on, but even so, we got around."

"Although there were restrictions about camping and access to parts of the area, we in fact got out and about with SBS in the Scouts and, of course, if you got roped in on one of his bird photography or bird study projects. I once helped to build a hide in woods near our house with SBS and Mr Thompson so that they could photograph some sparrow hawks on their nest. It was good fun, but Mother got a bit fed up because they would call in for tea and ate our butter ration!"

"I was on a Junior Walk once down by the Adur, with SBS leading it, when he found a rather good footprint of some bird or other in the mud. He took out a pencil and stuck it in nearby so that he could relocate the print to photograph or to make a plaster cast. Anyway, a bit later a senior overtook the walk and told SBS that he had found and rescued a pencil which some idiot had stuck into the mud. SBS was not very happy!"

"Listening to us, you would have thought that we were not that interested in the war! In fact, I think that we were, but only to a certain extent. I do remember, vividly, the rush to be first with the morning papers in the Common Rooms and 'bagging' pictures and articles by drawing a line round them and writing your name on the line. The arguments over that paled to insignificance when you found that someone else had bagged something on the back of the thing you had claimed! Of course it was not just war things we were after. A pin-up girl was more than fair game!"

"Even so, it was a bit of a game, wasn't it? You know, 'Hey, Rostov has fallen and they say Kharkov is about to as well. We seem to be winning!' Or 'Berlin's had a hell of a pasting and we've got the whole of the Mareth Line now. Whoopee!'"

"True, but what I think of when the Common Rooms are mentioned is shove-ha'penny football! The table in Big School was our Wembley Stadium, well polished and with the notches showing where the goals were. You had a smooth ha'penny as the ball and two pennies on each side as the players and used a ruler to shove them, taking turns."

"That's right and it was best if your goalie was a new penny which was heavier and had a rougher surface than the old, smooth penny you wanted as your attacker. Your goalie needed to be solid and difficult to budge whilst your attacker needed to float nimbly into action like a Stanley Matthews. We had some good games. That table is still around. The last time I saw it was in Long Dorm."

"There was quite a lot of informal music-making, you know. The school never had much of a reputation for music, but a number of boys played instruments with varying degrees of skill. Some were pretty good. We listened to records too."

"Peter Woolf was fine on the piano or the organ and he always reckoned that the church organ in Steyning was one of the best in Sussex. The other person who was proficient was Den Moss. He used to practice the clarinet on the train and inspired Norrie Cox to take it up. Norrie had his own trad jazz band in the USA. Den was a world famous saxophonist and played with all the top bands, although he was known then as Danny Moss."

"Most were not in that class! Johnny Scragg confiscated McCarthy's mouth organ on the grounds that he was doing a service to music lovers! McCarthy was furious and called him all the names under the sun – once he was out of earshot, of course!"

"Toasting slogs on the gas fire in Dormer Common Room was my favourite pastime. It kept you warm and improved the slog!"

"I can imagine! Then there were the quizzes."

"Quizzes? I don't remember those."

"Not question and answer quizzes, but when people had something they didn't want which was still too good to bin, they held it up and shouted 'Quiz' and the first to say 'Eggho' got it. Can't imagine why those words were used."

"Oh dear! The academic reputation of Grammar Schools is on the line here! Didn't you do Latin?"

"Well, yes, but it was just a year with Larynx Harris."

"Say no more, but your education can start again here. In Latin 'Quis' means 'Who'. To this can be added, as understood, almost anything and in this instance the phrase 'wants this thing' is the notional attachment. The answer 'Ego' means 'Me'. Easy, see?"

"By the time the 1950s arrived," I said, "We added the word 'decent' after 'ego'. The reason was that older boys though it a joke to hold up a bag which you hoped could be sweets, only to find out that it was rubbish. 'Ego decent' meant that you wanted it only if it was a genuine offer of something reasonable. If you found on getting it that it was OK but you didn't want it, you 'quizzed' it in turn. It was always felt a bit of a disgrace to the originator if something was 'quizzed' round the room and eventually binned. I even saw things being rescued from the rubbish bin because of that. We could be sensitive flowers, you know, unlike you war-hardened veterans!"

"In fact, the war did affect our education in one way. It played havoc with the normal leaving times and quite a few ducked out of school earlier that they would have done to help the war effort. I did myself, but then got back later into full-time education. Others went into munitions factories, but a lot of these early leavers were farmers' sons who went to help on the land. Ian Hardisty reminded me that he lost a good deal of school time because he helped out on a farm when labour was short and then left when he was 15. Turner was another who left early to help on his parents' farm."

"It wasn't just that which gave problems. I had a real struggle at home over things like homework. It was for ever 'Why don't you come and help with things? If you did your work properly at school, you wouldn't have to bring it home with you.' They were proud that I was at the Grammar School, but didn't know what it really meant to be a schoolboy there. They felt I was slacking and being unhelpful around the house when they were under a good deal of strain. Handing in poor prep to someone like Scraggy was a bit grim. Of course, you never felt like explaining why it was so poor. That would have been a bit like sneaking!"

"Well, things changed a bit after the war when the staff turned over with quite a few leaving and others coming back, or new masters arriving after being de-mobbed. Willie Goble ran Holland House a bit as though it was an Officers' Mess in the RAF. The return of Bill Lewis as Holland Housemaster was like a bucket of cold water being poured over you. Back to normal!"

CHAPTER 10

The Play's the thing!

Before 1936, the school did put on plays, but these had to be enacted outside the school. In 1936, as a part of the building programme, a combined Assembly Hall and Gymnasium was opened. At one end was a stage, behind which was a changing room with showers and with two doors opening on to the back of the stage. In morning Assembly, the staff occupied the stage and glared collectively at their natural opponents for the day who were standing in form rows across the Hall. Beneath the stage was a storage area used for the folding seats which were brought out and set up for the audience at Speech Day or for the School Play.

Richard Mathews, transformed things on his arrival. He came to teach Maths, but his heart was in the theatre. Although the stage was of reasonable size, an extension platform was constructed in 1938/39 which could be put up quickly for the Plays to give the extra space needed. New front, stage and wings curtains were bought, together with their runners and the metal structure needed to hang them and support the lights. The lights themselves were hired from Strand Electric in London and were the most up-to-date available. The only drawback was that the stage lighting amounted to some 15,000 watts and the electricity company had to fortify the fuses each year to take the load. Stage costumes were hired from Drury's of Brighton, a professional costumier. In a very short time, the school productions went from the undoubtedly amateur to the near professional.

Over the war years the following plays were put on:

Richard of Bordeaux. 1938.
Charles the King. 1939.
Traitors' Gate. 1940.
Tobias and the Angel. 1941.
Macbeth. 1942.
The Importance of being Earnest. 1943.
She Stoops to Conquer. 1944.
Busman's Honeymoon. 1945.
Twelfth Night. 1946.

This quite varied selection was tackled with enthusiasm and to good reviews in the local papers. With the exception of *Richard of Bordeaux* in 1938, where Richard Mathews, who later became a professional actor, took the lead and *Charles the King* in 1939, where Bill Lewis took the part of a pamphleteering lawyer who had both ears cut off (what a way to treat your maths master!), all the parts were taken by boys. For many, these were defining moments in their lives and the importance of taking part in developing not only a love of drama, but also personal confidence, should not be underestimated. A few did go on to become professional actors; others became professionally involved in direction, scenery and other behind-the-scenes work. For most, it is simply the pleasant memories of being involved as actors or backstage workers which endure. Members of staff were, of course, in overall charge of production, scenery, lighting, costumes and make-up, but the boys formed teams under their direction to erect and change the scenery; to operate the lighting and other stage effects; and there were the pressed-labour gangs who put out and put away the seats for the audience. There were also the more carefully chosen ushers for the actual performances.

For the School Plays, the producer was always a member of staff. Richard Mathews in the late 1930s, followed in 1939 and 1940 by Bill Lewis. Frank Bowman was producer through the main part of the war and Willy Goble then took on the job when he arrived to teach English in 1944. Frank Bennett was the usual stage manager and the woodwork master and art teacher headed up the construction and painting of scenery. Over-enthusiasm in the painting squad under Freda Sage's direction explains why parts of the gym floor showed signs of paint which lasted well into the 1950s! Make-up from 1940 onwards was done by Mrs James, the wife of the woodwork master and, after her marriage in 1943, Jean Scragg became involved and remained so until John Scragg's retirement in 1968. Some of the property was hired, but the Steyning shops were raided for antique furniture and things such as fire irons and china. In The Importance of Being Earnest, the tobacco company Abdullah is credited with providing the cigarettes. To be given free cigarettes which could be smoked with impunity, on stage and in front of your Headmaster was a popular perk no doubt to the relevant actors!

As with any enterprise of this nature involving public performance, boys and the natural hazards to be found backstage anywhere, there were moments of unintended excitement – an electrified fairy in a later production of *A Midsummer Night's Dream;* the loss of a costume during a quick change; the catastrophic over- performance of a sound-effect (or its non-performance); the split tights; the trip over a sword; the loss of lines; the moustache coming adrift in mid speech; the collapse of the steps supporting the actor in a window scene; the appearance of the carpenter's hammer above the battlements as urgent repairs were made to collapsing scenery; all these were enjoyed. Most, it is good to record, took place in the dress rehearsal which the whole school watched, rather than in the public performances. When things went awry in the dress rehearsal, audience participation was likely and repartee between stage and the floor was frequently lively and witty – wittier often than the text of the play!

Of all the plays put on during the war years, it is *Macbeth* which has stuck best in the memory both of participants and audience. The reviewer in the School Magazine was highly critical of the diction; the lack of cuts; some of the costumes; the arrangement of the seating; the timing of the performances in relation to the local transport timetables; and Lady Macbeth's 'un-queenly slouch'. Ngaio Marsh in *Light Thickens* calls the play short and faulty. A lot of actors call it an unlucky play. It is, however, compact and quick-moving; is full of blood and witches and it appealed to its young cast and audiences. It also made a profit of £40 6s. 2d. which was given to the Duke of Gloucester's Red Cross Fund for sending parcels to British PoWs. In fact all the proceeds from the plays throughout the war years went to that fund.

All in all, there seems a general consensus that in putting on these plays, the school did a lot to foster a love of drama and an appreciation of literature.

"'The queen, my lord, is dead'. / 'She should have died hereafter; / There would have been a time for such a word. / Tomorrow, and tomorrow, and tomorrow, / Creeps in this petty pace from...'"

"For heavens sake, somebody switch him off! It's like being back in an English class!"

"You are just one of the uncultured masses! I quote superb literature and you carp and quibble. A shame on you! *'Hence horrible shadow! Unreal mockery, hence!'*"

"I see that you don't agree that it is unlucky to quote from *Macbeth*."

"At least you are showing signs of a rudimentary education now!"

"*Macbeth* was drummed into me by Johnny Scragg in class, I'll have you know, and he made me learn chunks of it by heart – including that speech which you were murdering. I must say in all seriousness, that I am glad now that he did. It got me interested in Shakespeare and I still enjoy *Macbeth* for all its melodrama. What started you off on all this quoting just now?"

"Richard Mathews cropped up in conversation and we were remembering the School Plays and what fun they were."

"That's right! Ticker Mathews was a good actor, wasn't he. Took it up professionally later on too. That first play he put on, *Richard of Bordeaux*, was pretty good and got praised in the local paper. Burchell told me that the play so enthralled him that he determined to become an actor – which he did eventually – and he and Ticker started the SGS Drama Society straight after the play."

"What was the next play? I recall *Tobias and the Angel*, but I think there was something in between."

"There must have been because *Tobias* was well after the war started and *Richard of Bordeaux* was before the war. I know that because *Tobias* had a peculiar effect on me. Even now I am a bit embarrassed about it! To this day, I have an extreme aversion for men dressing as women, because I was very attracted to the angel in the play and was most annoyed with myself, knowing that it was a boy dressed like a girl. I know that young people do get crushes on those of the same sex when they are growing up, but this was somehow different because it was the angel I admired rather than the boy playing the part. I know that it sounds irrational in retrospect."

"By chance, I can tell you who your heart-throb was! Michael Groom!"

"Oh, my Lord! A nice enough boy, but knowing now that it was him might even cure my guilt feeling!"

"I always thought that the school's pragmatism was illustrated superbly in the production of *The Importance of being Earnest*, in 1943 I think. It must have been about then anyhow, because there was a good deal of fuss about explosives in the school at that time. Ken Mason, the boy playing Algernon and who had just had his hair specially permed for the part, was caught with a couple of tear-gas canisters in his locker. By rights he should have been expelled, but punishment was deferred until **after** the play's performance and he was bounced out then!"

"If you look at the review in the School Magazine, you will find no mention of Mason! He had become a 'non-person' however good his performance."

"It takes a bit of doing to review a performance of *The Importance of*

Being Earnest without mentioning Algernon directly at all!"

"My own claim to thespian notoriety is small beer compared with that, but I did get a bit of a kicking when, acting my socks off as Superintendent Kirk in *Busman's Honeymoon*, I said 'Oh Christ' loudly when a key prop failed to work. The Powers That Be felt that our visitors in the audience should be spared impromptu comments of that nature, whatever the provocation!"

"I think that in spite of your efforts, the play was very well received and got a glowing review in the Magazine."

"The best review of all was given to the 1946 production of *Twelfth Night*. Everyone was praised and the hierarchy of the school decided to give special book prizes for the best character portrayal; the best depiction of a range of emotion; and to the best female impersonation. Guess who got the last one – Chris Passmore!"

"Those reviews were good fun at times! In commenting on *Traitors' Gate* the reviewer, whilst complimenting the actors and backstage staff, had a real go at the author for poor dramatic structure, muddled thinking and historical inaccuracy. He ended by saying that it would be refreshing to see the young actors in *Macbeth*. He got his wish the following year!"

"We seem to have gone full circle. What about the 1942 *Macbeth*? That was something!"

"In spite of the reviewer's comment the previous year, he was not kind in his remarks on the production. He must have had indigestion or something when he wrote it. Everyone and everything within range were brutalised from the arrangement of the seating to Challen's 'un-queenly slouch'! But I really enjoyed it."

"There was one near catastrophe when the Banquo's ghost illusion was almost destroyed. I think that 'Billy' Bowman was involved with his physics hat on, but there was a strategically placed area of painted muslin in the scenery wall. The idea was that at the crucial moment, Banquo standing behind the scenery, would be strongly lit and so would appear through the wall. It worked splendidly. Then, just before the first public performance some clumsy clot – was it Thompson? –was prancing about on the stage and ripped the muslin. Calamity! However, the kitchen came to the rescue with some cheese-cloth – though heaven knows where they found that – and Freda Sage patched it in and painted over it and all was saved. A good bit of fire-brigade work!"

"The production was memorable – and for several reasons – but I find it a bit odd that everyone seems to remember it ahead of any of the other plays which were just as good, or better. I do remember Challen as Lady Macbeth – he was very good – and Routh as The Thane. He carried it off well too. It was the odds and sods of costumes which stick in my mind best, though. Some would have been good on cave-men; the witches seemed to be in cassocks; some people had clothes better suited to the Mediterranean than to Scotland; there were helmets like saucepans; crowns like rather strange kettles; and swords which you needed an arm extension to draw with any kind of authority or military intent!"

"Dim Smith was not very adept with his sword. He was Malcolm, wasn't he, and he had this damned great sword – I suppose the idea was that it was a sword fit for a king. He really had to go for it to get it out of its sheath right at the end so he could wave it about, to the great danger of the multitude, as he invited everyone to his coronation."

"Little Wiseman had a sword as big as himself, too. They wanted him to have a small one, but he wouldn't wear it. He didn't last long in the play and Routh's thugs did the decent thing and slaughtered the infant prodigy quite early on. You could see he got a real kick out of it all in spite of that. I think he was the only person from Form 1 in the play, which gave him great kudos in their ranks. I'll bet that he remembers all about it still. Your first appearance on a public stage makes a real impact on you."

"Mine certainly did! When I was about eight, I had to stand on a chair and sing 'Danny Boy' at a party. It is seared into my soul, old chap. Seared into my soul!"

"I'll guarantee that the 'London Derrière' has never sounded like it before or since!"

"Well, Rawson as Macduff drew his sword to good effect one time! He nearly cut Jackers Routh's finger off in their fight at the end. There was blood everywhere."

"I was talking to Derek Rawson not long before he died, you know, and Jackers came up in the conversation. Derek asked if I knew where he was these days and when I said that he was living on the other side of Canada, Derek came back with the remark 'Good God! He didn't have to run **that** far to get away from me!' Both have gone now. Time does slip by."

"*Life's but a walking shadow, a poor player, / That struts and frets his hour upon the stage, / And then is heard no more; it is a tale / Told by an idiot, full of sound and fury, / Signifying nothing.*'"

"He's off again! Do you go along with that?"

"Well, no I don't. I can see where Shakespeare is coming from, but I do rebel at the thought that all that we and our contemporaries have done add up to 'nothing'. That is too bleak for me. I cherish the memories and especially of those who are dead now."

"That is a kind of life after death, isn't it, to be haunted by old companions? A sort of immortality in the mind"

"It's a haunting I don't mind – in fact, I welcome it. What was it that Rupert Brooke said about Canada? Something like *'There walk as yet no ghosts in Canadian lanes. At a pinch one can do without gods; but one misses the dead.'*"

CHAPTER 11

Doing your bit

D uring the war, people were asked to make sacrifices of many kinds to help with the war effort. They were also asked to undertake a variety of tasks where the opportunity was there. Some of these activities, such as joining the Home Guard or ARP, have been touched on. Others included bringing in aluminium pots and pans, ostensibly to be turned into Spitfires; collecting scrap metal; saving waste paper; 'Digging for Victory'; helping with farm work; destroying crop pests; and fund-raising campaigns such as 'Wings for Victory'. It has to be said that some of these activities were of doubtful value in terms of achieving what the Government said was their objectives, however, their value lay in giving those involved a sense of contribution and achievement.

There was a limit to what schoolboys could do. A full-time education leaves little space in one's life to fill with time-consuming work and when it comes to fund-raising from pocket money, no reasonable person could expect much willing co-operation. John Lloyd McCarthy's diary sums this up, when in commenting on Steyning's 'Wings for Victory' collection, he wrote that he regretted to have to say that he had not given a damn farthing since it had all gone on chips! A few boys did go the whole hog and, in effect, gave up their education to help on farms or in factories, but these were a small minority. Some projects, such as saving waste paper, were seized on by staff anxious to find suitable minor punishments. The 'Cleaning-up Squads' served a triple purpose – saving paper; keeping the place tidy; and, as reparation for antisocial behaviour, developing a sense of service to the community! Other activities, such as helping on farms and digging allotments, or in some case gardens for elderly people, were built into the school curriculum and could occupy a part of school hours as well as of nominally leisure hours.

The more enterprising boys managed to take advantage of some of the schemes aimed at giving advice to local farmers. A Ministry of Agriculture science unit was based near to the school. Its purpose was to advise on the conversion of downland to arable, but the boys found that the experts there could and would identify specimens of plants or animals taken to them. This gave enthusiastic young naturalists a supplementary source of help which could cover gaps in the knowledge of members of staff such as Stanley Bayliss Smith and Frank Bennett.

Without any doubt, the work mentioned most frequently by those involved was that done on farms. This can be split into two types: 'fire-brigade' work on local farms, for example to rescue crops which were getting smothered with weeds; and the residential farming camps, which got the boys taking part further afield. The School Magazines mention camps at Thakeham, Amberley, Long Compton, Wormleighton, and between Nuneaton and Coventry, these last three being in the Midlands. In 1946 Mr Bowman, who had run these camps, left and the Magazine suggests that the North Warwickshire camp was to be the last of its kind. In 1942/43 two Scouts, Geoffrey Mason and Den Carter, joined a forestry camp in Shropshire by biking from Steyning in two days, stopping at a hotel in Banbury on the way! Bikes were usually taken by train to these sorts of camps for local travel, but some boys preferred to cycle all the way.

In addition to these organised camps, several boys took the chance during holidays to work on farms near to where they lived. In common with those on the camps, they were paid 9d. per hour. It seems, though, that unlike the boys on the camps, the Ministry did not pay these free-lance farm workers a minimum wage for weeks when bad weather precluded work on the ground.

The school also worked an allotment on the edge of the Playing Field. This is often referred to as 'Mr Scragg's allotment'. There seemed no real sense of ownership by the boys. Small gangs of boarders were expected to work there on Wednesday half-days, as illustrated by the comment that someone had missed an hour's hard work on the allotment because he had a cricket trial, held that Wednesday afternoon. There were large vegetable plots attached to Coombe Court and a small garden which went with No. 7 Church Street and which contained a greenhouse. The School Magazine for 1941/42 notes that both garden and greenhouse 'have given much pleasure and profit' but no-one has mentioned that vegetables were cultivated here by the boys. Certainly the Dig for Victory campaign was not approached with sufficient seriousness to see the Headmaster's Lawn turned into a potato patch! There is an impression that gardening was more of a chore than a pleasure and was sometimes imposed as a punishment. In the early-mid 1950s the plots at Coombe Court were cultivated by the caretakers and in particular by Mr Nash, who was a keen gardener. The boys stole carrots and peas to eat raw, but we were never really sure who ate the vegetables. The crops were not big enough for the school; perhaps the staff and/or caretakers used them. On one occasion the boarders ate, or attempted to, the crop of currants which, together with the associated invertebrates, leaves and stems, was incorporated in a Sunday lunchtime jelly. This author gained some interesting beetles from this for his collection. The rest of Holland House was not so favourably impressed.

Gardening is something which a lot of Old Boys enjoy and it doesn't take much to start a conversation about the terrible difficulties of growing things under the inevitably extreme weather conditions all were experiencing. Onions had been causing trouble. First it was too hot and dry; then the wet cold summer had meant poor ripening; poor ripening meant losing a lot through rot when storing them. However, onions triggered off memories of more distant times.

"I have a vivid memory of what seemed then an enormous field of onions at Thakeham where a group of us on a farming camp in 1941 spent two weeks weeding the bloody things. When the onions ran out, it was on to carrots in an equally big field. The light relief was when an escaped barrage balloon trailed its cable across the onions, destroying quite a few and so lessening our work!"

"Yes. I do remember that and I found all that weeding a bit soul-destroying, I must say. However, I reckon we probably saved a crop which might otherwise have been smothered. If you let onions get too weedy you get only half-sized ones and carrots will just give up altogether."

"Do you remember the rats in that shed we all slept in? In the end John Scragg and SBS, who were with us, organised a rat hunt. All the holes we could find except for two were blocked and a hose-pipe led from Scraggy's car exhaust-pipe into one of the holes. We bashed thirteen of the things as they staggered out of the other open hole. Not bad, I thought."

"Do you know, I forgot that Johnny Scragg was with us. There was a rumour that he was chasing Mollie Lindfield, the farmer's daughter, come to think of it! However, he brought his cannon with him and shot enough pigeons for us to roast them for lunch on Sunday. I came to the conclusion that there is not much meat on a pigeon!"

"That's right! We made the oven out of a big biscuit tin covered with a thick layer of clay. It seemed to work well, but it dried the birds out a bit."

"I never roast pigeons myself because of that. I usually rip off the breasts and casserole them with brown rice, herbs and a good chicken stock. Delicious! The rest of the carcasses go into a stock-pot to make soup and stock."

"Move over, Gordon Ramsay!"

"It was on this expedition that I was allowed to have a shot with Johnny's twelve-bore. It nearly knocked me off my feet and Johnny creased up laughing."

"I know what you mean! That happened to me too when my Dad let me use his gun. I soon learnt to keep the stock very firmly pressed against my shoulder."

"It was better when we went on that camp in Warwickshire in the autumn that year to pick fruit. It was not as bad as the weeding and we were close enough to Stratford to go to see one of Shakespeare's plays at the Memorial Theatre. *Twelfth Night*, I think."

"No, I am sure it was *The Tempest*. I remember Ariel's plaster hair, for some unknown reason!"

"There was a canoe fight, wasn't there, on the river just by the theatre?"

"That's right. Patching got capsized and we spent the whole performance swapping seats with him so that none of the seats got completely soaked. We must have been mad!"

"I think that I am getting confused. The autumn camp was definitely harvesting corn and we were in a building in Long Compton. It was on this camp that we went to see *The Tempest*, but we went back to that area and it was on that one that fruit picking featured. There was a trip to Stratford then and *Twelfth Night* may well have been the play. The canoe fight was at this second camp."

"That was 1942, wasn't it? There were over twenty of us who went up by train with our bikes for local journeys like the ones into Stratford. 'Titch' Mason was a hero, weren't you, and cycled all the way, camping, so he said, beside a trout stream on the way! We used an old laundry of the Manor House in a tiny place called Sherbourne for a lot of the daily activities, but slept under canvas. However, I was not involved in fruit picking but in regular harvesting work. We did split up, of course in the early mornings to go to the farms allocated, so there would have been a wide variety of work being done. Anyway, I was only there for the first fortnight and others stayed for a full month and fruit harvesting may

127

have been done in those last two weeks. A couple of other things stick in the mind. I went by myself to the Rollright Stones at around sunset and have never forgotten the sense of mystery when standing amongst them as the sun went down. I also can hear in my mind my mother's comments on finding that I had worn one pair of socks for the entire, sweaty fortnight. I thought that she would be impressed by my economical use of clothing; she was, but not in the way I had thought she would be!"

"We went on yet another camp in Warwickshire, didn't we? Somewhere over towards Leamington Spa in 1944. I remember that one for two reasons: I was allowed to drive a tractor; and was much taken with the girls of the Women's Land Army. The local cider and the threshing machine made their impression too. The only trouble was that the girls seemed less impressed by me than I was by them. I suppose that the cider may have played a part there. When your knees seem to have a life of their own – or suddenly die the death on you when you are not expecting it - you risk damaging a good reputation."

"That presupposes that you had one to start with!"

"I would have gone on the camps just for the hell of it, but we also got paid. Nine pence an hour, I seem to recall. It was very welcome so we could buy things like the cider."

"That was another thing about that camp. For two of the four weeks we were there the weather was dreadful and we did so little that the farmers wouldn't pay us and we had to get the Ministry to chip in with their guaranteed minimum wage. We didn't lose out by much in the end."

"It wasn't just the bad weather that caused this. 'Billy' Bowman, who was organising things, said that the War Agricultural Committee had forgotten to let anyone know we were coming and that he had to tout for work, sometimes without much success. It was a bit of a let-down to find yourself weeding a flower bed when you had proper farm work in mind!"

"There was one camp over at Amberley. That must have been in 1943. It was all harvesting work with just horses, carts and us. No tractors. It was bloody hard and hot work and drinks of cold tea, which I found was a real thirst-quencher, were the order of the day – unless you could sneak off for a lunchtime pint of cold cider in a local pub! It was a happy camp as I recall it, with around twenty of us and we slept in tents and on camp beds provided by the Army. SBS organised the whole thing."

"I remember the last day best of all because of its odd mixture of events so far as I was concerned. Harvesting the fields of Sussex in the morning; an afternoon train journey to Croydon and a lovely hot bath at home; travelling by train from Croydon into London to hear Beethoven's Ninth at the Proms in the Royal Albert Hall; back home for a wonderful night's sleep in a real bed! On the way into London on the train, I glanced out of the window to see a buzz-bomb travelling parallel with the train and about five hundred yards away. Luckily, the train driver had also spotted it and brought the train to a halt. A few seconds later there was a big bang and the train shook. We got under way again and quarter of a mile further on passed the smoking site of the explosion amongst houses."

"Lucky escape there. It could have been a case of 'Titch' Mason, deceased! But the V1's only started in 1944 didn't they?"

"Yes you are right. I am mixing things up here with a later train journey!"

"That reminds me of a story I was told about the Steyning Flyer. Apparently in the black-out, the ganger from Steyning, Mr Stillwell, had to sit on the front buffers and keep a look-out for any holes in the track which bombs might have left. The train crept along to Henfield and then, I think, someone else took over and he got the next train back, doing a repeat performance to Steyning."

"That sounds to me like something from the first part of the war. Later on people didn't take things like that so seriously."

"I never went on one of these farming camps, but regularly took a job on a local farm to help the war effort – and get some pocket money! I enjoyed the work most of the time, but the greatest benefit to me was working alongside prisoners of war and finding out that they were not the ogres which the Media made them out to be. They seemed pleasant men who were happy to help you and talk to you. I'm not, and was not then, an intellectual kind of bod, but it did get me wondering how we would have got on with the Germans and Italians if politicians had not existed."

"You could make money in other ways too – not much I admit. I used to rush about with a flail made of twigs, swatting cabbage white butterflies. When you had a respectable bag-full, you trotted along to the Ministry of Agriculture office near the bottom of Burdock's Slope and got a few pence for them. I probably did more damage to the cabbages than the caterpillars would have done, but it was a bit of sadistic fun."

"The Ministry people there would have known at least whether or not they were cabbage whites. We used to take round weird insects which SBS couldn't identify and they usually came up trumps for us. I too collected the white things, but for a village competition. Once was enough! I had meticulously slaughtered the two white butterflies whose caterpillars eat cabbages – the large and the small whites. The other boys had murdered anything white which was butterfly size. There were some large whites and small whites, but the main cull seemed to be of green-veined whites and even female orange-tips, with the odd female brimstone thrown in for good measure. None of these harm cabbages, or indeed any other food crop. When I pointed this out to the organisers they just laughed and gave one of these ecological vandals the prize! Ignorant lot."

"There were better ways of making a bit of money. As a Scout, I volunteered myself and my bike as part of the Home Guard and ARP messenger service in the evenings. We had quite a bit to do and you did risk the odd bomb, but we got 3s. 6d. which was not to be sneezed at. It didn't help with getting prep done either!"

"I did that too and it could get a bit risky after dark when you had no lights and the road could contain unexpected hazards like loose bricks or bomb craters, but I only came off a couple of times."

"We were pretty keen on getting money, but I can't recall anything of the same enthusiasm when asked to donate cash to the war effort. There was that Wings for Victory appeal in 1943 with an exhibition in the Town Hall of weaponry and aircraft identification charts. It was good to be allowed to handle some of the things, but that was about it so far as I was concerned. The Steyning target was to raise £125,000 and they did it, but I doubt very much that the boys gave a lot, if anything, towards it."

"The school was a bit more generous than its pupils, although I don't think it was over the Wings for Victory collection. The profit from all the School Plays went to the Red Cross for their parcels to PoWs and that could be a tidy little sum of around £50."

"Well, I think that a fair summary of all this is that we pulled our weight when something a bit different was on offer, like the farming camps, or when there was a bit of money coming our way, but that money once gathered, was either spent immediately on the things dear to our hearts, or locked away in vaults of which Fort Knox would have been proud, to be so spent as the opportunity arose. Selfish, really, but the nuts and bolts of the war were pretty remote from us. It was a bit of excitement to add on to normal school life. Money was a different matter and there are few beings as mercenary as the average schoolboy!"

CHAPTER 12

When Death came visiting

Extract from a Steyning schoolboy's diary

"Monday March 8th
Periods today: Double Science – Going over exam papers. French –
ditto. Latin – exam on Vergil – lousy. Geog – Exam papers. English – free
period. Positions so far; Science 18th, 47 out of 100, French 4th, 70 out
of 90, Geog 9th, 43 out of 100, Geometry 20th? 19? out of ? Geometry
very uncertain. 2 passes one fail. Asked Beef [Mr Bennett] about my
Starman's and Razzo [Mr Ross] about my Interpreters [Scout badges];
I'm certainly trying. Last night there was a minor air-raid; we all went
down to Dormer Lower Corridor. Wallis and I played mouth-organs
and we generally had a good rag. We got three-quarters of an hour
extra in bed, just for that, getting up at 8.15. Breakfast 8.40, prayers
*9.10. Singing practice tomorrow. **A most ghastly thing happened up***
at the field in the dinner hour. They were rolling the pitch when
Norman fell in front of the roller, was run over and killed. There
was an immediate investigation lasting most of the afternoon. It
happened in the middle of the B game pitch. Poor chap! It must
***have been a shock for his parents.** I read a good bit of The Red*
Tapeworm. I played 'dog-fights' most of the afternoon. I went out at
5.00 for some fresh air and to post a letter. Saw the usual crowd – not
so bad as yesterday, though. But I saw the brunette with the bike again
– she certainly is good. Next time I see her I'll have a shot at it – I wish
I knew her name."

Here, sandwiched between the normal trivia of a school day in 1943,
are the bare bones of something which affected the whole school and,
in particular, those directly involved. During a war, Death is constantly
there in the background. When he steps out suddenly right beside
you, it is a different and terrible matter.

It was a perfectly normal school day and in the lunch break two
punishment details were sent up to the Playing Field. There was a
cleaning-up squad of juniors to pick up paper and other rubbish and
a group of some fifteen or twenty, mostly older, boys who, under the

eye of a prefect, were to roll a pitch using a one and a quarter ton roller designed to be pulled by a horse. This was all quite usual. The rule was that all the boys towing the roller had to be outside the shafts and that no-one should ride on the cross-piece in front of the roller. The rear cross-piece was used across its length by boys pushing, except where other boys were sitting to act as a counter-weight to the shafts. As the roller was on its way to the pitch, ten-year-old Paddy Burges-Watson, one of the little boys on this detail, who was sitting on the end of the back cross-piece, got his hand trapped between the roller and the shaft and was quite badly hurt. As the prefect was coping with a damaged and no doubt tearful small boy, the rest continued with the roller. Glancing up, the prefect saw twelve-year-old John Norman fooling about on top of the roller, running backwards to keep on top and pretending to be a slave-driver with a whip. He shouted to him to get down. In doing so, he tripped and fell in front of the roller, which was far too heavy for the others to halt. It travelled the length of his body, stopping only when reaching the back of his head and he was crushed to death in front of his horrified companions.

Canadian soldiers who were bivouacked on the Field ran to usher the frightened boys away and back to school and messages were sent to the police in the nearby police station and to the school. Little Burges-Watson had been abandoned and ran to his home, which was not far away. His hand was hurt enough for him to be taken to hospital, but fortunately nothing was broken. No-one other than him remembers his hand. It is interesting that he went on to be an internationally known specialist in battle trauma when this event has left such a trail of trauma behind it.

There was, of course, an inquest. This apportioned no blame to the school or the prefect in charge. The only safety issue was raised by John Norman's father who asked what would be done to prevent any repetition of the accident. He was given an undertaking that from that time on, no boy would be allowed to ride on any part of the roller. At no time did anyone suggest that the roller should not to be used again by the boys, or that a member of staff should be present if it was. It was **usual** for the pitches to be rolled in this way. The day was a perfectly normal school day – except for one stumble and ten seconds of horror, the memory of which has not faded in the sixty-six years which have now passed by.

There was a special Assembly at the school in John Norman's memory and when his ashes were interred in a churchyard near to his home on the edge of Pulborough, several of the boys attended, with the Head Boy, Geoffrey Mason, Rodney Cox, John's friend and leader of the Cubs Six he was in, and Stanley Bayliss Smith, the Scoutmaster, being the official representatives of the school. Then people went away; the tragedy slipped into the background of the school; and life went on.

For the boys in the punishment detail and indeed for some others who were not in fact at the scene, the trauma is deep-seated. During their hectic working lives, with the added commitments of a family to cope with in many cases, the trauma could generally be kept under cover as a half-forgotten pain. Then, in their retirement, with the family dispersed, these Old Boys began to reflect on what they had achieved; what had been left undone; and what still needed doing. Thus to Rodney Cox, John's close friend, there was unfinished business which he was determined to address. His opportunity to do so came when a Directory of the Old Boys of the pre-1968 Grammar School was produced in 2002, Rodney Cox saw the chance to seek the thoughts others who had been involved. After almost sixty years he was not absolutely sure of the exact location of John's grave and he wanted to find it to make sure that it had been properly looked after. He also wondered about John's family and whether there were brothers or sisters alive. If there was anything which he and others could do then this might help bring a better sense of closure and greater peace of mind. He just wanted to be sure that everything was all right. The first person he turned to was the Head Boy at the time, Geoffrey Mason.

"Geoffrey? This is Rodney Cox. I am hoping that your good memory will be able to help me. It is about John Norman who was killed by the roller in 1943. I was one of the roller gang and only feet away from him when he fell. It has been on my mind recently to check that his grave is tended and to see if there are living relatives. The problem is where to start. I can't be sure which churchyard his grave is in, but know that you were at the funeral and hope that you can put me right."

"Let me think! It was one of the little churches overlooking the Arun flood plain between Pulborough and Amberley. I would guess it was the one nearest to Norman's house which was at Marehill, but I can't remember the name off-hand."

"Just a minute. I have a map here. Let me see. The nearest is Wiggonholt, but Greatham is not far away. Otherwise there is Pulborough church itself...."

"No, no. It was not in Pulborough. You went down a track to it and it was out in the countryside."

"The only other place I can see which might do is Hardham, but that is on the other side of Pulborough to Marehill. Anyway, that has given me enough to be going on with. I'll drive over and search those three churchyards."

"I do remember that the grave was about half way between the church door and the east end and only a little way back into the churchyard, but you had better not take that on trust! Good luck and let me hear what you find. I would like to know."

A couple of weeks passed by before another telephone call was made.

"Geoffrey? Rodney Cox back again. I have hit a snag over John Norman's grave. I have looked at every gravestone in the three churchyards, but there is nothing there with his name on it. I need to know which churchyard to concentrate on now if I am to find out anything more and have put some photos in the post to see if you can identify the church."

"I got them this morning, thank you. I am not too sure because they look so similar and it was sixty years ago. This is going to take some work if we are to get anywhere. We also need to talk through just what it is we want to do if we can locate his burial place."

"Well, under the circumstances, I would like to see some kind of memorial stone put up. It would make me feel more comfortable to know that he has something there to be remembered by. I have a nasty feeling, though, that there are some ecclesiastical hoops to be gone through to do that."

"I'm sure that you are right! I do know that it wouldn't be cheap either. Nothing is these days! Do you think that there will be others who would contribute if we found that we could do this?"

"I would be very surprised if anyone in the roller gang has forgotten, or indeed most of those who were at the school when it happened, even if they didn't know Jan. We have the Directory now and could get in touch with the ones I know were there on the Field."

"Sorry! You mentioned Jan. Who is that?"

"I forgot you were so much his senior. We always called him Jan and his parents did too, because of his initials – John Anthony Norman. I've got back into the habit of thinking about him as Jan."

"I have had a thought. Your mention of the Old Boys' Directory just now reminded me that George Barker was involved in getting a gravestone refurbished, added to and re-dedicated in Steyning churchyard. It was for the Matron from the 1950s and there was an appeal to those who were boarders and who knew her. He could probably help from his experience here, especially on how to raise the money and how to negotiate the diocesan rules about gravestones. The other thing is that he seems keen on the school and its history – and his legs are a bit younger than ours! I am sure that leg-work is going to be needed here. Why don't I get in touch and see what reaction I get?"

"That is a good idea, if you don't mind making the effort. It would really ease the burden at my end to have a bit of help."

"Leave it with me and I'll get back in touch."

Such are their powers of persuasion that in the autumn of 2003 I found myself confirming on the ground that there was no gravestone in any of the possible churchyards and shortly after that, examining the archive copies of local papers for articles covering the accident and inquest. Moving down the road in Chichester from the County archives to the diocesan record office, the burial registers for the three churches were brought out and there in the Wiggonholt register appeared:

'Burial of ashes. Burial No. 194. Name: John Anthony Norman. Cremated in Brighton. Interred at Wiggonholt. 16 March 1943. Age: 12.'

So far, so good, but there was no plan showing where in the churchyard the burial plot was located.

To cut a long story short, a few weeks later Wiggonholt churchyard saw Geoffrey Mason, Rodney Cox, George Barker and Bishop David Silk, the priest in charge of the Amberley Wildbrooks churches, pacing out the burial plots to locate the right one, about half way down the nave and some ten yards or so from the church wall into the churchyard. Thanks to the fact that most of the graves have stones, the right plot was pinpointed. The actual wording to go on to the memorial stone was discussed at length, with Bishop David insistent that the date when it was put up be included as well as the date of the boy's death, so that future historians are not misled. A Requiem service was proposed for

8 March 2004. An appeal letter was also agreed and was sent out to all those for whom we had addresses and who were at the school in March 1943.

The next challenge was to see if there were living relatives, especially any close family to whom the burial plot would belong and whose consent was needed to put up a memorial stone. For all we knew, it may have been his parents' wishes that the grave be left unmarked. Another Old Boy, Roger Tilbury, was brought in to search data-bases for any Normans living in the Pulborough area and letters were sent to all of them, but without any positive results. A conversation with the local Press led to an article outlining the story and asking for any information about possible relatives. This brought the news that there was a brother born some time after the accident, but no-one knew where he was. Then a phone call came from someone who had remembered that a Mr Norman taught handicrafts at Christ's Hospital School, near Horsham, in the late 1940s and into the 1950s and he had a son at the school. This fitted with our knowing that John's father had been a teacher and Christ's Hospital confirmed that Eric Norman had taught there and that there was an Ian Norman of about the right age on their register of Old Boys. They passed my message on to him and in a very short space of time, we were in direct touch. By coincidence, Ian had been talking with his wife a few days earlier about trying to find and mark his brother's grave, but was put off by not knowing where to begin – then my letter had arrived like an answer to prayer!

Ian confirmed that he was born after John's death as a 'replacement'. His mother often spoke about Jan and said that he was a bit 'fey', immersed in wildlife and nature and making but little contact with people. He also revealed that Jan was conceived out of wedlock, although their parents married very shortly afterwards. For the best part of a couple of months, their father took the baby to friends in the motor-bike side-car whenever his parents visited, only presenting the baby as a rather mature 'new born' after a suitable lapse of time – nine months from the wedding. Thus were the decencies preserved, even though it is unlikely that anyone was deceived!

After this, everything went into overdrive as an appeal was launched; the money for the memorial stone collected and accounted for; the stone itself ordered; a memorial booklet written; the service sheet and Homily printed; the church booked; car parking arranged by Tim Ashby, an Old Boy, with a couple of his farm hands as attendants; and, thanks to Geoffrey Mason's acquaintance with the Headmaster of the day, Peter Senior, who lived in the same Suffolk village as Geoffrey, a buffet lunch set up in Long Dorm after the Service.

On 8 March 2004, a congregation of sixty people crammed into a church capable of holding fifty, there to remember; to look for comfort; and to hope for closure to that far off tragedy. By coincidence, Bishop David dedicated the stone, virtually to the minute, sixty-one years after Jan slipped and tripped.

In the short and moving service, Bishop David said: *"There is much to remember today, and before we disperse from the church this afternoon, many of us will want to share particular memories with others we meet, perhaps for the first time in many, many years. Memories make us what we are; memories are for sharing: the terrible things in our memory strengthen us; the rewarding things in our memory encourage us; and all memory contributes to our understanding, bestows upon us perspective and perception...........In a moment we shall together stand in a nearby garden, in the garden where John's mortal remains were interred, the garden of dying and the place of sorrow, regret and perplexity. But by the virtue of the rising again of Jesus the garden may also be the place of new life, new hope, of joy and confidence. It is there that we shall reflect on our response to the events of 61 years ago and of today. Our lives have been damaged by John's death, but repaired by the promise of his rising."*

Ian Norman, in his eulogy, said, frankly, that had the accident not happened, he, his children and grandchildren would not have existed: *"So what appeared to be the tragic, meaningless, end of a life in fact has proved to be the beginning of the story of eight new lives. Every action I and my descendants make, every relationship that we experience down through the ages stems from that moment. In little ways perhaps millions of people will be affected by that instant."*

In Long Dorm over lunch, the conversation was a bit subdued as people thought back across sixty-one years.

"Jan was a friendly lad, often up to mischief, but I think that this was him trying to make a mark. That was often why we did things. Just wanted to impress our friends!"

"I remember him as a most pleasant, quiet and gentle boy. Not much,

I know, but I would be more than happy to be remembered as that. Do you know, that was probably the first time any of us had really been struck by the thought of death."

"I know. It was as if a grey cloud had come down over the place. A stunned quietness descended over the school and its activities. I wasn't there on the Field, but I was absolutely stunned and shocked when I heard."

"I don't think that a lot of us believed it when boys came running in and started telling people. I imagined that it was just a rumour to begin with, but then someone who had been up there gave away his sandwiches because he couldn't eat them."

"Stuart-Clark got everyone together in a special Assembly and told us all what had happened. It was then it began to hit everyone and not just the ones who had been pulling the roller."

"I recall him as a bit of an oddity. He was keen on natural history, though, which got the approval of SBS. He brought a dead heron in once and kept it in his locker which was next to mine – then a prefect got wind of it and it was chucked out! I saw him drink ink too for a dare."

"He was not bad with his hands and his father taught handicrafts – metal work mostly I think. He made this little working model of the destination sign on the front of the bus which he could wind on to show the different place names."

"Yes. I remember that too."

"I suppose that it was SBS's interest in him which got me involved. I was a Sixer in the Cubs, which SBS ran and he put Jan into my Six and told me to keep an eye on him because as an only child, like me, he needed someone to look after him a bit. I was not too sure about his reasoning, because no-one had been told to take special care of me! It was probably that SBS saw him as vulnerable and easily led. I must say that although Jan was always cheerful, never quarrelling badly with anyone, it was sometimes hard to get him to concentrate on learning his knots and things like that and he always had his socks down round his ankles! I did count him as a friend, although he was a day boy and I was a boarder, and was only inches from him when he was killed. I was holding my hand out to him to help him jump down when he tripped on that front cross-piece and fell in front of the roller. There was nothing we could do to stop the roller; nothing. That still affects me, which is why I started all of this off."

" I'm glad that you did. It is odd, but I have been thinking about it more and more over the past few years. Strange that it should start coming back like that. It is good to have it all out in the open and with the rest who remember it to talk to."

"It really did dig in deeply, you know. I was not on the Field myself, but it gave me nightmares for a long time afterwards and even now it surfaces from time to time without warning. I don't know whether all the counselling which would have followed today would have been any help. We, of course, could only talk to each other and make the best of it."

"The school seemed to pull a veil across it all afterwards. It was never mentioned officially once the inquest was over. It was encouraged to fade from the general memory. In fact, when she first heard what we were up to, Jean Scragg said to Geoffrey, 'You surely don't want to start raking all that old stuff up again.' It was only when it was explained just why we wanted to do this – to set the ghosts to rest if we could – that she came over and was very supportive."

"At the time some people thought that John Scragg was to blame. He had sent Norman up to the Field for not wearing gym shoes in the gym when sitting an exam there and he was Duty Master that lunch-time and some said that he should have been supervising the roller gang, but it was always a prefect who was in charge of the lunch-time punishment detail. The Duty Master had everyone else back at the school to worry about; a couple of hundred or so boys, as opposed to the twenty up on the Field."

"My clearest memory of that day is of John Scragg's face as he raced up to the Field having been told the news. That and then seeing Matron coming along in a hurry with a sheet over her arm. They were probably more shocked than we were."

"I am not so sure. It happened shortly after my father died and it was at the height of the war, but it is my most abiding memory from my two years at the school. I was nine at the time."

"I agree with you. It has haunted me in private over the years. I was in the squad pulling that damned roller, but oddly enough I cannot now recall details of Jan or of how the school reacted. Undoubtedly I was suffering from a form of shock which is in a strange way still with me."

"He was a pretty happy-go-lucky boy and seemed not to have a care in the world. This may have contributed to his death. We really didn't realise how close to the edge we often came and why no-one got killed by explosives or by the other pranks we got up to – swimming in the Adur or in the clay pits, for example – only the Good Lord knows. Jan was the unlucky one who fell off the edge."

"It was only afterwards that I got to think about his parents. Of all the possible things which could have happened in the middle of the war, a fatal accident in the school lunch hour whilst with his friends would not have occurred to them in their wildest nightmares. I was so impressed by their dignity, mixed with grief, at the funeral and the total absence in them of any sense of blaming the school. It really picked me up today to meet Jan's brother, Ian, and find out that they had the later joy of a second son and of grandchildren."

"That is interesting from another angle too," I put in, "You know that we had enough money left over to buy a memorial seat to go on what we remember as the Headmaster's lawn. Well, Ian tells me that two of his grandchildren are going to Steyning and will be able to sit on a seat dedicated to the great-uncle whom none of them ever met. He says that this has tickled their fancy!"

"Well, I think that this reunion and the Service has been a great help. Although it was not a joyous occasion, I find it a very happy one. It has been so good to meet up with the many people I've not seen for sixty years. How we have changed in so many ways: but how unchanged we are in others!"

It is a quiet little churchyard. Few people go there and wildlife abounds. Jan would have liked it. His stone, a bit incongruous in polished granite amongst the older limestone slabs, stands as a reminder of a long-standing heartache amongst those who had it placed there for a friend.

IN MEMORY OF
JOHN ANTHONY NORMAN
11 DECEMBER 1930 – 8 MARCH 1943

WHO DIED IN A TRAGIC ACCIDENT ON THE
PLAYING FIELD OF STEYNING GRAMMAR SCHOOL
AND WHOSE ASHES ARE INTERRED IN THIS PLACE

THIS MEMORIAL, SET HERE BY HIS FAMILY
AND OLD BOYS OF THE SCHOOL,
WAS DEDICATED ON 8 MARCH 2004

"In the faith of Jesus Christ, and for the good of his holy Church, we dedicate this Memorial Stone to the Glory of God, and in the memory of his servant John; in the name of the Father and of the Son and of the Holy Spirit. Amen."

"Rest eternal grant to him, O Lord:
And let light perpetual shine upon him.
May he rest in peace.
Amen."

CHAPTER 13

The end in sight

D-Day was planned for 5 June 1944, but stormy weather delayed the invasion of Normandy until the following day. Very early on 6 June, the Airborne Divisions dropped into France and by 6.30am the first sea-borne troops landed. During the night, aircraft had been dropping strips of foil ('window') in the Calais area to bluff the Germans that we were trying to conceal an invading force. Further down the Channel during the night, an exercise in precision flying was in progress to make the German radar posts detect a slowly approaching landing fleet which did not exist. With the RAF now totally dominant over southern England, the Luftwaffe had been allowed to photograph only what the Allies wanted them to. This included the east coast areas where dummy landing craft and gliders appeared and inflatable 'tanks' were positioned to suggest that Pas de Calais was a target and, in fact the Germans thought initially that the Normandy landings were cover for the main landings at Calais. Meanwhile, the trees of the New Forest gave cover to more substantial weaponry than the east coast held.

By this time, the whole of the south of England was, in effect, a military camp. Everyone – including the Germans – knew what was going to happen. The only questions were 'When?' and 'Where?'. Even the big secret projects were known by most people - the Pluto pipeline for example, prepared a year before to carry oil supplies under the sea to the beachheads. Some of the preparations were on such a huge scale that no-one in the vicinity of them could help but notice. The Mulberry Harbours work is a good example – but what were they for? Rumour suggested that the enormous concrete caissons were supports for nets in which to catch submarines! In fact they were, of course, parts of the floating harbours which were towed across the Channel so that supply ships could be unloaded readily.

Even in Steyning there were signs of the troop build-up and movement. In the nearby south coast towns such as Littlehampton and Shoreham, these signs were clearer. In the countryside around, boys had watched aircraft practicing 'snatching' gliders from the ground and the battle-training areas on the Downs were heaving with activity.

So, what was going on at the school on 5 June 1944 to support the D-Day landings? A group of boys under the direction of Stanley Bayliss Smith was carrying out dawn to dusk observation of a goldcrests' nest in a yew tree in the garden of Coombe Court. The feeding schedule of the birds was much more important than the war! In the context of the school, someone had got their priorities right. Ornithology was accompanied, however, by the thunder of hundreds of planes flying overhead on their way to France. The boys had a pretty good idea of what was going on, which was soon confirmed in news bulletins.

The euphoria over establishing a bridgehead in Normandy was dented when the first doodlebugs arrived on 12 June. The strange sound of the ram-jets and the fiery trail they left at night puzzled people at first, but the new threat was soon recognised. The attack by 'pilot-less planes' was announced officially four days later. With a typically British eye for the essential, the Cabinet met and decreed that these contraptions should be called 'flying bombs'. That adjustment made, we could get on with the war.

The conversation had meandered along the highways and byways of memory but now sat down to rest for a moment around D-Day.

"I got quite excited seeing the build-up of troops and equipment. We all knew that it meant the invasion of continental Europe, but of course, no-one knew just what was planned or when anything would happen."

"That's right! The thing I remember best was the tanks rumbling down the street. Some came from the station right past the school and shook the whole place."

"I was in the Sea Scouts and cycled to Hove for a meeting. The whole front was crowded with the Guards Armoured Division when I went by, but the whole lot had vanished by the time that I cycled back. Then, from my bedroom window I saw a mass of planes towing gliders heading out to sea and knew that things had started. It felt good."

"I'll second that! Even before we really knew that the invasion was on, it lightened the mood seeing the constant stream of military vehicles heading for the coast. It meant that after years of defence, we were on the attack."

"I watched the Commandos at Chantry Green fixing snorkels to their jeeps so that they could be driven off the landing craft without the water affecting them. Later I found out that this was a general order throughout the invading force, but it puzzled me at the time."

"I was with a gang down at the Iron Bridge off Kings Barn Lane when a great wave of aircraft flew over. The air shook with their noise and there were so many that we knew that something special was happening."

"I was at home then and knew that the landings were about to start when that mass of aircraft went over in the evening light."

"It was before D-Day that I was on a bike ride with a pal just north of Ashington when we saw gliders making practice landings. They were repairing gliders there too. At the end of the airfield there were poles like rugby goals and they would put a wire across with a loop. The wire was attached to a glider and then a Dakota would fly over trailing a catching line and, if all went well, whisked the glider into the air. All very exciting so far as we were concerned!"

"All of that could well have been aimed at the battle for Arnheim Bridge, you know. That happened after D-Day, of course."

"I think that Arnheim was in September 1944. That seems to stick in my mind. Anyway, it was a while after the Normandy landings in June. I do recall seeing the sky filled with aircraft towing gliders well after D-Day and have always imagined that this was the Arnheim attack getting under way. It was in between D-Day and that moment that the doodlebugs started."

"That was weird you know. The first time any of us saw them was at night on a farming camp. There was a funny noise like a badly tuned motor-bike and these red dots of flame in the sky. All I could think was that they were aeroplanes which had been hit and were on fire. It wasn't until later that we found out what they were."

"Steyning was off the main 'bomb alleys' and we didn't have all that many coming over. What we did have was enough and the boarders had to suffer the air raid shelters from time to time. Somewhere like Lewes saw a procession coming over all the time."

"We did get a few, as you say. I was playing in a cricket match on the Field when we heard a buzz-bomb coming and Mr Moore, who was umpiring, held his arm out to stop me running in to bowl until it went over safely. I was told that it came down in Amberley Wild Brooks and killed some horses."

"There was one which I watched as it flew more or less along the line of the Downs near Steyning. Heaven knows where that one came down."

"We used to see them coming over the sea and the RAF fighter pilots tried to shoot them down before they crossed the shoreline. After that, the risk was that the things could be shot down over populated areas."

"I must say that the idea of trying to shoot down a flying bomb does not really appeal to me! However, those boys must have known what they were doing. I once saw a pilot get his wing under the wing of one and try to flip it over or jockey it round to go back out to sea. That must have taken some skill. It worked too! The thing came down in the water. I wonder whether he got a medal for that – he deserved one!"

"It seemed like no time at all to me between the D-Day landings and VE Day, but it was quite a while really, I suppose."

"Best part of a year. D-Day was in June '44 and VE Day was early May '45. I remember that because of the parties, which meant extra food!"

"The school laid on a feast for the boarders and you were allowed to invite local girls. This was very much a 'first', but, alas, also a last, apart from an annual dance. The dances were usually a bit of an ordeal with the staff acting as gooseberries."

"I think that your view would be endorsed by the humorist at Christ's Hospital who ensured that their annual dance appeared in the rugby fixtures list as 'Dance v. St Catherine's, Bramley'!"

"I'd agree that one or two of the local maidens would have been at home on a rugby pitch, but some were more than OK! Who got Jane Gray at the VE Day party?"

"I am pretty sure that Kitchener won the jackpot there, because he often mentioned the follow-up. Apparently the boarders were allowed to escort their partners back home and had 15 minutes grace after midnight to do so. Kitchener set off with Jane, who lived somewhere near Penn's House on the Horsham Road. He got back to the school at 2.45am and found, to his horror, SBS and his fairly recent wife were still up. He had been praying 'Let them be dead' when he realised the time, but it was not to be! His excuse that he was sorry, but he had not realised that the fifteen minutes grace were over, was a bit thin, but he got away with it thanks to the general euphoria around the surrender of Germany."

"That's what I remember about it, that feeling of jubilation. It was as if a weight had fallen from your shoulders. It shows that we did know that there had been a war on, however much we seemed on the surface to ignore it."

"We seem to have forgotten the ultimate celebration of VE Day. The *Daily Mirror* undressed 'Jane' completely, having spent the war tantalising everyone by nearly, but not quite getting there! It gave another meaning to the term 'strip cartoon'."

"Trust you to remember that!"

"That was all in early May, but the war went on with Japan until August."

"We didn't seem to be that interested. It was a war between the USA and Japan so far as I was concerned, even though our troops were involved."

"I am pretty sure that we didn't really know just what devastation the two atom bombs caused in Hiroshima and Nagasaki. I know that I had in mind some vague idea that it was like a rather concentrated normal bombing raid."

"I was at a West Sussex County Council Youth Camp when the word came that an atom bomb had been dropped on Japan. As you say, we had no real idea of what that meant. Then there was the second bomb a few days later and eventually the surrender of Japan. Compared with VE Day, VJ Day was a subdued affair."

"I owe my life to President Truman! I'm convinced of that. I was all kitted out and aboard the troop ship to sail for Japan when those bombs dropped. Yes, I reckon that saved me at least."

"I was still at the school having only arrived there in 1944. On VJ Day it so happened that I and another boy – I can't recall who it was – were on a 20-mile hike for a Scout badge. There was a tremendous feeling of joy and freedom knowing that the war was at last over and here we were on a lovely sunny day, on top of the Downs and walking towards Washington."

"There you are! As I said, the war did get to us rather more than it appeared to on the surface."

"There are depths to me, old chap, which people don't appreciate."

"From what little I know of you, my boy, those are depths which I do not wish to plumb!"

CHAPTER 14

And afterwards?

It was natural, although highly optimistic, to expect things to change for the better once hostilities were over. They did not. They got worse. People were tired and even the General Election of 1945 was greeted with remarkable apathy, especially amongst the Forces where over 50% did not take up their postal votes. A Labour Government was returned and set about the job of trying to improve the lot of the poorest households. Working Groups during the war years had met and set out the foundations for several Acts which have lasted in one form or another to the present day – the Planning Act, The National Parks and Access to the Countryside Act, The Education Act amongst them. However, the immediate job was to get the country back to some semblance of order while at the same time demobbing some five million people from the Forces and conscripting others to fill the vital gaps.

Angus Calder in *The People's War* summarises the position:
*'The Japanese surrendered on August 14th. On that day, a minute for the cabinet emanated from J.M. Keynes in the Treasury. Britain, he said, was faced by a 'financial Dunkirk'. Lend-lease, sure enough, was terminated abruptly. With external disinvestment amounting to four thousand million pounds; with her shipping, an important source of invisible exports, reduced by thirty percent; with her civilian industries physically run down after six years of war and her visible exports running at no more than four-tenths of her pre-war level; with 355,000 of her citizens dead by enemy action at home and abroad; with bread rationing looming ahead and spirit and flesh rebelling against further effort, the nation could consider only wanly the good fortune which had spared her the destiny of Germany, or Russia, or Japan.
As for her imperial pretensions, they were finished.'*

That paints a bleak picture, but the fine detail, illustrated by people's comments at the time, presents an even bleaker one. I have here mercilessly pillaged David Kynaston's *Austerity Britain. 1945-51*.

'We are in an awful MESS', wrote Vere Hodgson, a sentiment endorsed by a north London schoolteacher who felt that *'Dreariness*

is everywhere. Streets are deserted, lighting is dim, people's clothes are shabby and their tables are bare.' You still could not buy the coloured crockery which prevailed before the war, but it was the lack of food which gave rise to the greatest discontent. As long after the war as 1949, a combination of mismanagement and dock strikes led to the meat ration being reduced because supplies from Argentina were not getting through – and the queues grew outside the horsemeat shops! The black market flourished as never before, even two bishops were overheard discussing how to get hold of extra things through it! Certainly the vague wartime thought that you were somehow letting the country down by using the black market, vanished after the war to be replaced with the happier thought that if the Government wasn't going to look after you, you were entitled to help yourself.

The severe winter of 1947 disrupted transport and froze potatoes into the ground where they had not been lifted or into clamps if they had been. Coal was in short supply thanks to a combination of transport problems and disaffection amongst the miners following nationalisation of the mines and as a result restrictions were brought in on the use of electricity. It was industry which first bore these, but soon no-one in London, the Midlands and the north-west could use electricity between 9.00am and 12.00am and between 2.00pm and 4.00pm and this was extended across the nation shortly afterwards. TV programmes, the Third Programme and many magazines were suspended; restrictions were brought in on broadcasting times for the Light Programme and the Home Service; lack of newsprint meant smaller newspapers; street lights were turned off; and there was no electricity for events such as greyhound racing; shops and offices used candles and nightlights. Contravention invited a £100 fine or three months in prison. Kingsley Amis writing from Oxford to a friend, summed up the general feeling across the nation quite simply, *'Christ, it's bleeding cold!'*

Where food was concerned, the basic ration now included both potatoes and bread, neither of which had been rationed during the war, and several items already rationed had this ration reduced. In 1947/48 the bacon ration was 1oz a week and you also got 3lb of potatoes, half a pound of bread, 2 oz of butter, 3 oz of margarine, 1 oz of cooking fat, 2 oz of cheese, 1 lb of jam or marmalade a month and one shilling's worth of meat a week which was reduced in 1949 to eight pence worth. Fresh fish was in short supply and the attempt

147

in 1947 to enliven the culinary market by introducing a tinned South African fish called snoek was not a success! On the plus side of things, particularly where children were concerned, sweets came off the ration in April 1949, but only to go back on ration in August because demand far outweighed supplies! To schoolboys it was the disappointment of a false dawn! Even Government Ministers were not immune from making caustic comments. Aneurin Bevan said *'This island is made mainly of coal and surrounded by fish. Only an organising genius could produce a shortage of coal and fish at the same time.'*

It was not only the limited supplies of food which struck visitors from abroad, but also what we did to it. Ronald Reagan, over here filming at Elstree, wrote *'What they do to the food we did to the American Indian!'* Egon Ronay looked for the reasons and concluded that *'The people who influenced food at this time had been to public school, where the food had been not just without interest, but horrifying. So you did not discuss food.'* The humorous and satirical magazine *Punch* joined in with some glee: *'"Excellent meals can be obtained if you know where to go," says a correspondent. He claims to have found a restaurant where food is fully up to war-time standard.'* Another quip from *Punch* was *'"Fry your whalemeat with an onion to absorb the oil," advises a chef, "and throw away the onion." As well?'*

All in all, Tennessee Williams' remark *'I guess England is about the most unpleasant, uncomfortable and expensive place in the world you could be right now'* was fair enough. Certainly this glimpse of the Welfare State in action did not impress Ronald Reagan who gained the view that no-one was well and everyone was doing badly. It influenced his political thinking and he said later that he shed then the last ideas he had of government ownership of anything. Be that as it may, a study comparing the diet of four-year-olds in 1950 and in 1992 concluded that the 1950s diet was the better one.

However, the National Health Service, which began on 5 July 1948, did offer something to the poorer households, but here as with other initiatives, it was the middle classes which came off best. The Education Act of 1944, which affected the school directly, not only raised hostile comment from those who felt that grammar schools should not be replaced by comprehensives, but also failed in one of its main objectives – to get more people from poorer families into university. In the 1950s, while one in seven children from middle class families went to university as opposed to one in sixteen in pre-war years, for the poorer families the proportion stayed the same. T.S. Eliot voiced sentiments which are still sounded today. *'In our headlong rush to educate everybody, we are lowering our standards.'* This thought was certainly shared by the Headmaster and Governors of Steyning Grammar School and underlay the later opposition to the school being incorporated in a comprehensive school. However, the introduction of the 11+ examination did let the grammar schools cream off the academically brightest children, which was the intention. The Secondary Modern schools, Technical schools and comprehensives all lagged behind.

It should be noted that when a Conservative Government came to power in 1951, it did not change the policies it had inherited from Labour in any radical ways, but rather expanded and extended them.

When the effects of hygiene and education on the world today are glanced at, one is tempted to go along with Mark Twain when he wrote: *'Soap and education are not as sudden as a massacre, but they are more deadly in the long run.'* However, while the nation seemed to be covered by some sort of shabby grey cloud, what was happening in the school?

The School Magazine for 1945-47 says *'Out of school activities have increased considerably during the last two years.'* This is substantiated by a list which included Art Exhibitions, a Music Society, Scouts, Cadets, Walking Tours, Farming Camps, Summer Camp, School Plays, Chess Club, Radio Club, Gallery Club (theatre and film shows), Philatelic Society, Modelling Club, Debating Society, a visit to Belgium and a joint visit to Scotland with boys and girls from Quorn which was reported in an illustrated article in *Picture Post.* Thanks to the generosity of Mr Breach who allowed the use of his tennis court, a Tennis Club was started. There were school dances too and the Magazine reports that girls from The Monkey Club came to these. When the soldiers left Wiston House, a girls' finishing school took over and it was called The Monkey Club! Oddly enough, given the boys' interest in girls, when the Debating Society looked at the benefits of co-education, this concept was defeated heavily!

There were other changes too. Founder's Day was shifted from the summer term to the Easter term and Speech Day substituted for it in the summer. A half-term holiday was introduced in the mid-1940s to allow boys from farming families time off to help on the farms. This also meant that the boarders no longer endured the long separation from their families which an unbroken term gave. In 1947 a programme of regular film shows was instituted for the boarders (and any day boys who wished to come). Cissa House was reinstated in 1948. The school had grown considerably since 1938/39 when Cissa House was discontinued and there were enough boys now to fill another day boys' House and still leave the three with not many fewer members than the boarding House, Holland.

An attempt was made to demolish the air raid shelters in the playground and with economies in mind, John Scragg used his connection with the local Forces to get them to do it for nothing. The Sappers attacked the shelter nearest to the primary school with pneumatic drills and the noise was indescribable. After impassioned representations from the primary school's headmaster, work was switched to Saturdays, but was then abandoned until the early 1950s. Unknown to the boys, the Commandos were invited during the holidays to demolish a blast wall outside the kitchen of Holland Cottage, the Headmaster's house. This they did using plastic explosives. The wall was destroyed; windows were blown out on Dormer landing; and the Scragg's first-born, baby Cathie, was terrified! There were other problems too. The Library was unable to get up-to-date atlases because the post-war boundaries to countries had not been finally decided!

The end of the war also saw several of the masters retire or move on and an influx of younger teachers replace them. Eric Moore (gymnastics and general subjects) retired in the spring of 1946 and was replaced by Idris David. Major Child and 'Razzo' Ross retired in the summer of 1946 and were replaced by 'Tommy' Thomas and Keith Sorrell respectively for science and French and 'Barrel' Clover arrived to take on general subjects with the junior forms. Harry Collison (geography) left in 1947 to take up the headship of Bishops Stortford Secondary Modern School and in the summer of 1947 Messrs Bowman and Chaplin also left. The first of the new staff, Tom Pretheroe (maths and physics), had been appointed in 1944 and 1946 saw the return of two of the pre-war staff, Bill Lewis (maths) and Dennis Lovell-Clark (classics and English). The following years to 1950 saw many staff changes with Bill Lewis being replaced by Bernard Jones both as senior maths master and boarding Housemaster; Idris David being replaced by Frank Potter for a year before the post of PT master was filled by Bob Webster. Ieuan Williams replaced Thomas as biology master in 1950; Paul Coltman took over English from Willie Goble also in 1950; and the previous year Bill Gardiner replaced Lovell-Clark as classics master. 'Spud' Crannigan had come in 1948 to take the junior forms in French after Capt. Palmer Stone left. 'Oink' Orton taught history from 1947 until 1950 when Arthur Lee took over. 'Sockless' Rendell taught geography for the same years and was replaced by Doug Harvey.

These movements saw some changes in the out-of-school activities where the enthusiasm of key members of staff had kept things going (for example Messrs Bowman and Collison with the Cadets, which faded away once they left) and where new blood brought with it a fresh enthusiasms (for example Bill Gardiner's interest in archaeology which gave birth to the Archaeological Society). This flurry of staff movements may give an impression that the average length of stay was short at Steyning. If so, this impression is false. Steyning had the reputation of a school in which staff stayed for long periods of time; a reputation borne out by the statistics.

It was not just the staff which changed and was supplemented in the five years following the war. The buildings were too. The acquisition of the whole of Coombe Court, allowed the two gardens and two halves of the building to be integrated to give a boarding house with two classrooms incorporated. The school now also included Wykeham, a house in School Lane, as another addition to the accommodation for boarders and with it a pleasant garden with one of the oldest mulberry trees in the County. By 1951 a new physics laboratory had been built between the woodwork shop and the gymnasium. In 1950, a new Playing Field had been prepared alongside the Horsham Road on the edge of town and the Cricket Field by the police station handed over by its committee to the town as a memorial Playing Field. The school was on the move!

Back at the school the mood had changed to fairly lively from fairly solemn in the church. We had returned from Parish Communion and the re-dedication of Astrid Andersson's gravestone with the additions made by former boarders who had known her first as Nurse and then Matron. She came to us in 1946 from The Monkey Club and remained until her death from cancer in 1964. It was 2003 and it was the first large gathering of Old Boys from the pre-1968 school for very many years. Inevitably, the past was being mulled over and dormant memories roused from their decent slumbers.

"Were you at the school when Bill Lewis came back as Holland Housemaster? He was teaching maths before the war and after a spell in bomb disposal was a stretcher-bearer in the Parachute Regiment – not exactly sinecures for a conscientious objector! More to the point so far as I was concerned was his rather cold and formal manner. He could be a bit frightening with those icy grey eyes staring at you."

"He was only there in my first year and he had us all out on cross-country runs before breakfast. The bugger came too and carried a cane! Anyone towards the back of the field when we got to the Horseshoe was encouraged along with flicks of the cane. Luckily I could run quite fast."

"Well, what about 'Pecksniff' Jones who took over from Bill Lewis in 1948. I'd back him against Bill Lewis as a grade 1A frightener. 'What is this, boy? What is this?' used to send shivers up my spine as his hand clumped your head."

"Do you remember the end-of-breakfast announcement 'We will see the boy so-and-so in our study at ten to nine'? It was always the royal plural! If your name was in the hat, you knew you were for it. Three of the best as a minimum and he could lay it on!"

"If he asked you a question in class which you were slow to answer, he made you stand up and came up to you and would pat the back of your head – not all that gently either – and say 'think boy, think!' Of course, all sensible thought left your brain in an instant!"

"Don't I know it!" I said, "But we did get one good laugh from that habit when he picked on Martin Ford in my class. Martin was around six foot six when he was eleven. When Jonah got him to stand up he was out of range for the head-patting and was commanded to 'Sit down boy. We cannot reach you.'"

"There was another good moment which I liked. 'Minnie' Mansell's parents had been summoned to the school to discuss with Jonah Minnie's continued poor behaviour. Now, they had only heard Minnie call him 'Pecksniff' and assumed that it was his name. When they came in at the staff entrance, evil fate arranged for Jonah to be walking through the hall and they asked him where they could find Mr Pecksniff. There was a brief and glacial pause, then, 'I am the person you want and my name is Jones'. Double trouble for Minnie!"

"Jones was a boffin in the war, wasn't he? Worked on things like bomb-sights. Applied maths, I suppose, and he went on from us to Loughborough which specialised in engineering and other applied sciences involving maths."

"I don't know about that, but I do know that the resident junior masters were as much in awe of him as most of the boys. Do you remember John Godfree who spent a year in charge of Coombe Court and taught general subjects? He told me that Jonah warned him off going drinking in the Norfolk Arms with Bill Gardiner and 'Spud' Crannigan. He told him that 'sins abound in the Norfolk Arms'."

"Now Crannigan was not one to be scared of Jones! He was absolutely no respecter of persons, but a damned good teacher from our point of view with a lot of good yarns to liven up the French periods. I heard that Jones asked him to bring cigarettes back with him from the pub and that Spud forgot and drank the money!"

"A case of 'We will see the man Crannigan in our study at ten to nine'!"

"I can tell you what the outcome was of that, Jonah would grab a junior boarder to fetch the fags instead. Of course he couldn't go into the pub and so was dispatched to the Tuck Shop. For some reason, he always called Cummings, who ran the shop, 'Mr Dogsbody' and so the instruction would be 'Go to Mr Dogsbody's and bring me twenty Players – two packets of ten.' When you got back, there were a few minutes of mental arithmetic to be played over the change on the basis of, 'And if the price of cigarettes was x, how much change would we have? And now, if the price was y, how much change would there be? Now suppose that there had been a box of matches at z, how much change?'"

"In my time," I chipped in, "It was John Lewis who was the favoured shopper for cigarettes. Once, Jonah beamed at him at said 'Very good, boy! Very good! Come with me,' and led the way up the stairs to his study. He drew out a bunch of keys and sat down at his desk. A drawer was unlocked and a cash-box extracted. 'Great,' thought John, 'I'm going to get a tip.' The box was unlocked and a packet of Maltesers brought out: 'And a sweet for you boy!', as a single specimen was handed over. John has puzzled for years why the packet of Maltesers was being kept under conditions more secure than those devoted these days to confidential Government papers!"

"Do you remember his daughter? I think her name was Margaret, but no-one called her that. She must have been in her twenties and was a substantial figure. In fact, to put it bluntly, her boobs were king-size! A slang term for 'breasts' was 'bristols' and the biggest aircraft constructed in Britain at the back end of the forties was the Bristol Brabazon. She became known as the 'Bristols Brabazon', always abbreviated to 'The Brab'. Even Jonah joined in the fun sometimes and called her 'Brabazon'!"

"Come to think of it, quite apart from being younger and, on the whole, more enthusiastic than the war-time staff, the ones who came in after the war were just as odd in their own way as their predecessors. There was certainly no lack of characters. You can count Tom Pretheroe in amongst the post-war staff, after all he came in 1944 and lasted right through to 1968. Then there were 'Barrel' Clover, 'Wog' Rendell, 'Spud' Crannigan, 'Digger' Gardiner, all as crazy as blue jays, and later 'Shocker' Webster and Arthur Lee to add to the mix."

"I thought that Keith Sorrell and 'Percy' Coltman were pretty sane."

"The exceptions which prove the rule!"

"We always called Rendell 'Sockless' because he wore no socks, especially in the summer, but you called him 'Wog' just now. That is new to me. Did he come from the Middle East or something? I never associated that with him for all that he was a bit of a religious nut."

"No, no! Nothing to do with that! He took charge of a Scout camp at some point and in an introductory speech to the troops said that since he was a good Scout with a woggle, they could call him 'Wog'. At this point, a voice filled with mock awe was heard from the back 'Golly! Wog!'"

"Good grief! Political incorrectness piled upon political incorrectness! Wasn't it about then that the school Play was *Ten Little Niggers?*"

"That's right. It was put on in 1949. Someone told me that the idiots have changed the title now to *Ten Little Indians* or some such. Next thing they will be changing the first book in the Bible to *Origins* because *Genesis* is too close to *Genitals!*"

"No good! *Origins* is too close to *Organs!*"

"A lot went on then, of course, which would be beyond the pale now. Even the sorts of things which Tom Pretheroe said to us would be barely acceptable They did upset a few sensitive flowers then, but most of us almost egged him on to come out with some of his sarcastic remarks. I do remember one which showed that he had small powers of prophecy. Bill Bushby was a fine footballer and Tom saw him day-dreaming in class and guessed that the First Eleven was in his thoughts rather than mathematics. 'Pay attention, Bushby,' he said, 'You can never earn a living out of playing football.' How much a week do the top guys get these days? Just a bit more than the total of Tom's life savings, I'd hazard!"

"There was this running joke too, over Rod Warrington's prep. Rod was hopeless at maths, but his father could cope with a lot of his prep work and did so. It took Tom about five seconds flat to realise the situation and when the exercise books were returned with the prep corrected, we would get the drawled comment 'Ah, Warrington, kindly tell your father that when calculating the area of a circle…' or, 'Warrington, while your father is perfectly right in his answer, his proof is defective in one particular…' Best of all was when everything was right and in his book was written '10/10. Congratulations, Mr Warrington. You have a fine grasp of the subject – such a pity that this was not passed on to your son.'"

"Lovely! I'd not heard that one."

"Bill Gardiner could make you sit up too by doing the unexpected. When he first arrived, we tried him out to see how far we could go. I was in Remove and Hall, a great long thing, was at the heart of the strife. Bill was only knee-high to a flea and went marching down the room towards Hall, dragging a chair behind him. Hall was told to stand up and Bill climbed on to the chair to stare more or less eye-ball to eye-ball with the boy. 'Now look here, Hall, this just won't do.' The class laughed with him rather than at him and he had no trouble with us thereafter."

"Do you know," I said, "I think that from what I have heard, the masters enjoyed it themselves when things went awry. John Moore, who preceded John Godfree as a resident master briefly – marriage claimed both of them and there was no space for a married resident master – once told me that before a class, he set up an elaborate system of levers and pulleys in the lab. He demonstrated this, accompanied with his words of wisdom, to a middle school class. So far, so good, but he then, without thinking, put the end of the pulley cord into his pocket and walked away. As he said, the results were fantastic. Chaos and disaster. Brilliant! Now, you do not recount a story against yourself like that if you had not enjoyed the outcome! Boys did not have to mess about always to see the gratifying humiliation of teachers."

"One who we did rag was Clover, but he could lose it if you were not careful and once or twice really laid into a boy. Didn't you know him? Must have been just before your time then. His nickname of 'Barrel' was descriptive and he favoured a haircut with very short back and sides and with a sort of crest of dark hair on top. He would set you some fiendish problem in maths to solve and then go into a kind of trance, smiling softly to himself and walking up and down the classroom between the desks. As he walked he would hold his hands out, palms down and with his fingers extended as if examining his nails. With every pace he would bob his head and hiss. Any slight stir from the class brought the admonishment 'Quit the shindig, brats' or more usually, just 'Shindig, brats' which was adopted by some as another nickname."

"Sounds as nutty as a fruit cake!"

"Not really – just a schoolmaster."

"Talking about oddities, how about Captain Palmer Stone, old 'Pumice-stone'?"

"Just how he survived as a resident master for so long, I will never know. I suppose it was a case of not talking about things like that to the other adults in charge, because they would never take your side – or so you thought. He was there throughout the war and only got bounced out by John Scragg in 1948 when someone did complain."

"Are you talking about what I think you are talking about?"

"Let me put it like this. One of his catch-phrases, much imitated, was 'Where's the soap, boy?' He would appear at bath-time to drop a bar into the bath, ask the question and then 'help' the boy concerned to find it. That was only part of it too. Then, one day he was summoned from the class he was teaching; was given an hour to clear his rooms; and we never saw him again."

"Most of the boys simply took evasive action and treated it all as a pretty normal part of boarding school life, but others were very badly affected and the scars endure to this day."

"The plus side to this sad tale is that when he left, 'Spud' Crannigan arrived to take over his job as a French teacher and resident master. He was berthed in No.7 Church Street, rather than in Dormer where Pummy had held sway."

"Now, that I did know! I was one of two senior boys in a tiny dormitory in No. 7. One of our jobs was to make sure that Spud was awake in the morning after a session in the Norfolk Arms the night before. We also got the benefit of his highly entertaining company in the evenings before he heard the siren call of beer. The main problem with that berth was the fire-drill. It had the merits of brutal simplicity. You chucked your mattress out of the window into Church Street and leapt out after it. It was a long drop, but if you executed a neat forward roll, you were more or less in the Tuck Shop!"

"Do you know," one said thoughtfully, "If you could put the school we knew in the 1940s into a time-machine and drop it intact into the present day, I reckon that all the staff would be in prison and all the boys being given counselling! And we never gave any of it a thought. It was just taken that this is how things were and you coped."

"There is too much protection given to kids these days, as well as all that stuff about political correctness. It can't do any good. Take all this nonsense about never hitting – or caning – a child, for example. I don't believe in really belting a boy, but physical correction is natural – just look at adult mammals with their youngsters: a badger or a lion will cuff a misbehaving cub; a cow will butt a naughty calf; and as for monkeys….! When it comes to caning, we have ritualised things, but it did show us lads where the boundaries were to what was socially acceptable and what was not."

"All that may be so, but the thing that I recall is that just after the war we began to go on trips again, including some abroad. There was one to Belgium, with Willy Goble in charge, which was especially good because there were things in the shops there, like chocolate and fruit, which we had not seen for years or which were rationed. I'm sorry to say that little of my booty actually got back home – other than inside me. The temptation was just too great and in any case my money ran out."

"If things were bad in England, they were worse in Germany. One Old Boy exchanged a few cigarettes for a big brass microscope and prepared slides which he brought back and donated to the school. I don't know what happened to it, though."

"Well, I can tell you," I said, "Because we were still using it for 6th Form biology in 1957/58. It was called 'Big Bertha' and the lenses were good. Unfortunately, the ratchet for focussing it was worn and the thing had a tendency to run down on to your slide and could break it if left unchecked. I think it was retired in 1958/59 because of that and in any case the school bought some new microscopes then."

"I missed the trip to Belgium, worst luck, but did go on a later one to Paris which Keith Sorrell organised. We were in a pretty cheap hostel, but we found out that it was close to the Moulin Rouge and sneaked in right at the back, which was all we could afford, to see the *Folies Bergère*. We were miles from the stage and were pretty disappointed. Then a gang of American sailors turned up next to us and, being experienced campaigners, they had brought the ship's telescope! They were generous enough to share it with us and so we felt we had got our money's worth from our dip into the night-life of Paris. Sorrell would have blown a gasket if he had known!"

"Poor old Sorrell. He took a holiday job once in a hotel to earn the money to take his family on a good holiday. You can guess what happened. One of his pupils turned up with his family to stay in the hotel! These days everyone would have laughed it off, but then it was embarrassing all round."

"The member of post-war staff who had the biggest influence on me was 'Oink' Orton."

"Oh yes, I remember him well. An Austrian Jew wasn't he, who had come to England before the war to take a History degree at Oxford. He served in the Army and came to us once demobbed. The problem was that he was so enthusiastic about his subject that he rattled away in a pretty thick accent and I found him hard to understand. Nice man, though and he used to help out with the Scouts. He moved on to Radcliffe College and, I think, stayed there until he retired. We then got another enthusiast to teach history, Arthur Lee. His English could be quite basic when the mood took him, but you never had any difficulty understanding what he had said!"

"Although I enjoyed 'Oink's' history classes, it was his thoughtful and balanced discussions about religion which got me interested and led me eventually to Catholicism. Now that really was a life-changing gift! Totally unexpected too."

"Steyning did not really go in for religion much, although individual members of staff were involved privately. Given that, I'm always surprised to see how many Old Boys went into the Church."

"Well, given John Scragg's antipathy for Eggie Bill, I wonder that we were subjected to so much exposure to services each Sunday! We had lots of other preachers in our evening service in Big School, but never him!"

"Who the hell is 'Eggie Bill'?"

"Did you never call him that? The Reverend Ceredic Egerton-Williams, vicar of Steyning. There was a story going round the parish that if on his first visit to you he was offered a whisky he would come again regularly, but if you offered a cup of tea, that was the last visit you would get. I don't know whether there was any truth in it! Johnny Scragg made damned sure that he left the matins service before the sermon, but left us to endure it."

"I do remember being marched down to the church in pairs with the prefects walking alongside the column. When Johnny left the church, they were left in charge, but on the whole turned a blind eye to what you were doing unless it was too obvious and was attracting attention from the rest of the congregation."

"A good number of us left our mark on the pews, myself included, I am sorry to say. I think about half of the 1940s boarders have scratched their names there. When I went to have a look the other day I noticed that most of the people I remember as prefects had done so – so they could scarcely complain if they saw us making our mark for posterity."

"All the same, I think that it would have been your posterior which would have gained a few marks, rather than posterity, if Johnny Scragg had seen you at it!"

"Present company excepted, prefects could be bastards! On my first day as a boarder a prefect sent me out at the tea inspection to clean my shoes. I hadn't the faintest idea what I was supposed to do or where I could find any shoe-cleaning gear, so I just gave my shoes a rub with someone's blanket in Long Dorm and went back. Then I got told off for sitting down without reporting first to the prefect who had sent me out!"

"Oddly enough precisely the same thing happened to me on my first day – and it was you, you sod, who sent me out! No pity; no remorse either, I see from the way you are doubled up laughing! Mrs Miller, I am relying on you to take your unrepentant husband down a peg or two for inflicting cruelty on small and innocent boys."

"'Small' I will grant you: 'innocent', never!"

It was some time after what became known as 'Matron's gathering', that a smaller group of older men stood in Big School looking at the war memorial tablet to those Old Boys known to have been killed in the second world war. To them, the names inscribed were not simply names, but in many cases were of friends and class-mates who died as young men, but who were for ever boys in memory.

"It took a long time to see that put up, didn't it?" said one.

"Indeed, and if it hadn't been for Jeff Turner coming over from Australia in the 1990s, there might still have been nothing."

"How come?"

"Jeff was quite upset to find that the WW2 casualties were recorded only in a rather tatty typed list pinned up under the WW1 memorial. He wrote to the local paper about it and galvanised the school and several Old Boys into action. As a result, this tablet was set up. From what I gather, the tablet was put on hold after the war because no-one was sure that all the Old Boys who had been killed were listed. Then no-one thought to take it off hold. Instead, efforts were concentrated on getting Old Boys to subscribe to a memorial library of books about Sussex. It ended up as a set of Sussex Archaeological Society books and ten volumes of Sussex poets. I suppose you could say that this is the equivalent of the war memorial gates for WW1 at the old main entrance to the school in the Brotherhood Hall tower."

"I subscribed to the library, in fact only Old Boys were allowed to do so, but what happened to it? Do you know?"

"Yes, I do. It is still there in a memorial case in the headmaster's study here on the Church Street campus. There is an inscription *'Presented by*

Old Boys as a memorial to their comrades who fell in the War 1939-1945'. We could take a look later if you want to."

"Yes, I would like to see it. It seems a pity that it is so tucked away. I wonder how many people know it is there and how many have actually used it."

"I'm afraid that people don't use books now in the way they did when we were young!"

"It was one of the worst experiences of the war, you know, hearing that someone you remembered as a senior had been killed. Most of the time all the fighting seemed little to do with us, but then you found that one of your school heroes had died. I was really upset when I heard about Claude Mitchell. It was my ambition as a new boy to get him to go 'snags' with me in playground cricket and sometimes he was kind enough to agree. It was hard to imagine that I would never see him again."

"He was unlucky. He died at the end of May 1945 with the end of hostilities in sight. No-one knows what happened. He was flying off *HMS Colossus* on the east coast of Africa and simply didn't come back."

"Now there's the name of one whom I remember well as a thoroughly decent young man who was very kind to a young boy. Harold Baker lived near to my family in Steyning. He was a turret gunner in Blenheims and the plane was shot down over Belgium. His body never has been found."

"Frank Martin was a bit of a hero, wasn't he? He was killed when working on bomb disposal and was awarded a posthumous George Medal. We do know where his grave is; it is in Cuckfield cemetery. Incidentally, the memorial tablet has the date wrong. I know that he died in 1940 and not 1941. He was relatively old too, having left the school in 1934."

"Wisden Stenning was another good one. Very keen on all kinds of sports and fit as hell! He was shot down in December 1941 and has no known grave, but his name I know is on the Runnymede Memorial in Panel 52."

"George Grigg I remember. Do you know, his father was hit hard by his death. The heart and drive seemed to go out of him and he no longer took such an interest in his grocery business. I expect he had hoped that George would take it over from him."

"Look! There is one who really ought not to have been there at all. Johnnie Grantham was wrapped up with his horses. I'll swear that they could talk to each other. All he wanted from life was a quiet time riding horses and even as a kid, he had won major prizes. What he got instead was the rank of sergeant air gunner; fifteen months as a rear gunner in Stirlings; and a fiery death when he was unable to bale out with the rest of the crew when the plane went down in flames over France. That was in May 1944 and it was six months before the family found that he was buried in a cemetery in Poix."

160

"What was it that Owen wrote? *What candles may be held to speed them all? / Not in the hands of boys, but in their eyes / Shall shine the holy glimmers of goodbyes.*' Come along. We are no longer boys and I'm afraid that all of our regrets will not prevent future wars for one instant."

"Perhaps so, but we can always hope – and even when memories are tinged with sadness, they are worth hanging on to."

"Do you know, now that time has rattled on I envy them in a funny sort of way. I find myself putting the wrong emphasis to Binyon's line so that it comes out *'Age shall not weary **them** or the years condemn'* – especially when I feel tired and creaky."

"Now then! After all that we have done we are entitled to feel tired and creaky. I reckon myself lucky to have had a good life and doubly so to have had such a good start by coming to the school."

"Hear, hear!"

Nostalgia and gratitude are inextricably mixed in the minds of most Old Boys from the years covered in this account. In noting change, there is too a desire to acknowledge continuity. *'I still visit Steyning,'* wrote one Old Boy to me, *'And day-dream – the Penny Drink Shop, the Tuck Shop, the café where we ate on sandwich days, the market, the station all gone! But Church Street, Big School, the Headmaster's House all remain – and behind the school's locked doors, small ghosts still roam free in the corridors and classrooms of memory to laugh, study, play and to tease a hundred be-gowned and spectral masters.'*

If ghosts there be, they mingle with a present-day crop of children which, in its turn, will look back over the years with a smile and, no doubt, mild disapproval at the young people of the day. The school, set up nearly four hundred years ago to cater for not more than fifty boys, now holds around two thousand boys and girls. William Holland would be astounded and delighted to see how today's young students are carrying on the traditions of the place and, amongst their many other achievements, are keeping alive the high standards of learning and good behaviour which were his hope in endowing the school. Certainly their predecessors from the 1940s wish them well in facing the challenges of an increasingly daunting world.

Almighty God, our Heavenly Father, we give thee our humble and
hearty thanks for William Holland, and others our benefactors, by
whose bounty this School was endowed for the promotion of godliness
and sound learning, beseeching thee that we, using these gifts to thy
service, may be, with them, partakers of thy Heavenly kingdom;
through Jesus Christ, our Lord.
Amen.

Steyning Grammar School. A special prayer on Founder's Day.

References

Angell, Stewart. 1996. *The Secret Sussex Resistance 1940-1944.* Midhurst, Middleton Press.

Anon. 1936-1950. *Steyning Grammar School Magazine.* Steyning, Steyning Grammar School.

Barker, George. 2001. *The Slog Smugglers. A Boarder's-eye view of Steyning Grammar School in the 1950s.* Peterborough, George Barker.

Barker, George (ed). 2004. *Dear Jack…..: Letters to Jack Routh in response to his short memoir of Steyning Grammar School in the War years.* Peterborough, Steyning Grammar School Old Boys.

Barker, George. 2006 (amended electronic version 2008). *What's in a name? Nicknames given to members of staff by the boys 1920-1968.* Peterborough, Steyning Grammar School Old Boys.

Barker, George and Tilbury, Roger. 2008. *Making a mark. Names of former boarders inscribed on pews in Steyning church.* Peterborough. Steyning Grammar School Old Boys.

Blaker, Nathaniel. 1919 (Revised from a 1906 document). Reprinted 2007. *Sussex in Bygone Days.* Bakewell, Ashridge Press/Country Books.

Brown, P.P. and Scragg, J. 1948. (Third edition). *Common Errors in Gold Coast English.* London, Macmillan.

Calder, Angus. 1969. (Pimlico edition 1992). *The People's War: Britain 1939-1945.* London, Pimlico.

Cockman, George. 1987. *Steyning and the Steyning Line.* Steyning, Wests Printing Works.

Coltman, Paul. 1974 (Revised 1982). *Weald and Downland. Poems by Paul Coltman.* Worthing. Flexiprint.

Davies, Jennifer. 1993. *The Wartime Kitchen and Garden: The Home Front 1939-45.* London, BBC Books.

Garratt, John G. 1973. *Bramber and Steyning. With notes on Beeding, Coombes and St Botolphs.* Old Woking, Unwin Brothers Ltd.

Grigg, C.A. 1967. *Memories of Steyning.* Steyning, Wests Printing Works.

Ford, Harry. 1980 (revised 1990). *Steyning Conservation Area Guide. A pictorial walking trail.* Steyning, The Steyning Society.

Hogg, Jane, Kettleman, Tony, Neves, Val and Tod, Chris (eds). 1993. *Steyning at War.* Steyning, Steyning Museum Trust.

Ivatt, Ian. 2000. *Food for Thought: Wartime in Steyning.* Steyning, Steyning Museum Trust.

Knight, Katherine. 2007. *Rationing in the Second World War: Spuds, Spam and Eating for Victory.* Stroud, Tempus Publishing.

Kynaston, David. 2007. *Austerity Britain 1945-51.* London, Bloomsbury Publishing.

Longstaff-Tyrell, Peter with Patricia Berry. 2002. *The Maple Leaf Army in Britain.* Polegate. Gote House Publishing.

Ministry of Information. 1945. (Introduction 2007 by Richard Overy). *What Britain has Done 1939-1945. A Selection of Outstanding Facts and Figures.* London, Atlantic Books.

Sleight, J.M. 1981. *A Very Exceptional Instance: Three Centuries of Education in Steyning, Sussex.* Worthing, Gadd's Printers.

Sleight, J.M. (ed). 1999. *Schooldays Remembered: Recollections of Steyning Grammar School 1840-1960.* Steyning, Steyning Museum Trust.

Warwicker, John. 2008. *Churchill's Underground Army: A History of the Auxiliary Units in World War 2.* London, Frontline Books.